Glimmer
& other stories & poems

Rowan B. Fortune
(editor)

Cinnamon Press

Published by Cinnamon Press
Meirion House
Glan yr afon
Tanygrisiau
Blaenau Ffestiniog
Gwynedd LL41 3SU
www.cinnamonpress.com

The right of the contributors to be identified as the authors of this work has been asserted by them in accordance with the Copyright, Designs and Patent Act, 1988. © 2010
ISBN 978-1-907090-17-2
British Library Cataloguing in Publication Data. A CIP record for this book can be obtained from the British Library

All rights reserved. No part of this publication may be reproduced, stored in a retrieval system, or transmitted in any form or by any means, electronic, mechanical, photocopying, recording or otherwise without the prior written permission of the publishers. This book may not be lent, hired out, resold or otherwise disposed of by way of trade in any form of binding or cover other than that in which it is published, without the prior consent of the publishers.

Designed and typeset in Palatino & Garamond by Cinnamon Press
Cover design by Mike Fortune-Wood from original artwork: Debutante Collage by Tamara Kulikova, supplied by agency: dreamstime.com

Printed in Poland

Cinnamon Press is represented in the UK by Inpress Ltd www.inpressbooks.co.uk and in Wales by the Welsh Books Council www.cllc.org.uk.

Introduction

A good short story should not be a microcosm of the novel—the medium has unique characteristics that make the writer choose it. In Tonya Mitchell's winning story of Cinnamon Press' tenth competition anthology, *Glimmer and Other Stories & Poems,* the medium is not incidental. It utilises the abruptness, succinctness and intensity of the form to create an apt structure for a narrative centred on remorse and guilt and it elicits a feeling of pathos that is difficult to capture in prose. The Romanian-French aphorist Emil Cioran said that, 'A book should open old wounds, even inflict new ones. A book should be a danger.' That is what Mitchell's story achieves.

David Underdown's winning poetry explores uncanny moments, places, raptures and events. '3 a.m.' is elegantly simple, evoking restless insomnia with those details about which we become hyper-aware in the sparseness of night, 'distant house lights blink and tremble,/ dance through drifting veils./ Inside a silent presence of machines,' He opens with the fitting metaphor, 'Those nights when sleep leaves you stranded,/ a sand-bound hulk on the bed/ of a long gone sea.'

Despite being the best, both of these authors are representative of the quality of the collection as a whole. As with the last three competition anthologies I am privileged to edit this selection of contemporary writing.

Rowan Fortune-Wood
Tŷ Meirion, August 2010

Contents

Glimmer by Tonya Mitchell	7
3 a.m. by David Underdown	14
7.10 a.m. Friday 16 October 2009 by David Underdown	15
Fathers and Sons by David Underdown	16
Lichens by David Underdown	17
While we slept by David Underdown	18
Null by Viccy Adams	19
On The Night of a Full Moon by Sue Moules	23
On Seeing a Framed Paper Nautilus by Marina Sanchez	24
View by Marina Sanchez	25
The Hide at Minsmere by Marion Ashton	26
The Halt by Jane Draycott	27
Fathoms by Sharon Black	32
After Skye by Sharon Black	34
My Parents' Bedroom by Sharon Black	35
Onset by Sharon Black	36
Flutter by Sharon Black	37
The Way Back by Bridget Thomasin	38
Soup by Jane McLaughlin	39
Road Edge Poem by Graham High	45
Snowy Day by Martin Willitts, Jr	46
Letter from Chopin to George Sands, 1847 by Martin Willitts, Jr	47
Letter from George Sand to 'beloved little corpse' by Martin Willitts, Jr	48
Night Boat by Will Kemp	49
Kesteven by Will Kemp	50
The startled deer by Will Kemp	51
This Ride Goes Backwards by Rachel Crowther	52
Woman sitting in the sun by Lynne Taylor	63
The Brutalist School by Gavin Goodwin	64
Woman at a Window by Gavin Goodwin	65
Pretty Woman by Eabhan Ni Shuileabhain	66
Bilocation by Eabhan Ni Shuileabhain	67
The Buddha's Footprint by Cassandra Passarelli	68
End of the day in the wood engraver's studio by Philip Madden	74
Halley's Comet Visiting Rights by Philip Madden	75
Piano from Mars by Philip Madden	76
Achilles in the farmyard by Padraig O'Morain	77

Cut-throat by Padraig O'Morain	78
Not talking by Padraig O'Morain	79
The fool's journey by Padraig O'Morain	80
Bodies in the machine by Padraig O'Morain	81
Candyfloss and Doughnuts by Kate Brown	82
The Biography of Dorothy Edwards by Aisling Tempany	91
Welsh writing in English by Aisling Tempany	92
Because the Revolution will not come by Aisling Tempany	93
The Captayannis by Marion McCready	94
Child by Marion McCready	95
Life Rafts by Marion McCready	96
Heading For The Coast by Lizzie Fincham	97
Collected Love-In-The-Mist Seeds by Lizzie Fincham	98
Two Sheets by Lizzie Fincham	99
Rule of Thumb by Amy Shuckburgh	100
Games by Lyn White	108
Westerbork Transit Camp by Lyn White	110
Gull by Lyn White	111
Klompen by Lyn White	112
Trace by Frances-Anne King	113
Lost Constellation by Frances-Anne King	114
Roman Uncle by Frances-Anne King	115
Bart's at Five a.m. by Frances-Anne King	116
August on the River by Jane McLaughlin	117
St Anthony at Baiardo by Jane McLaughlin	118
Twilight's Baby by Sue Vickerman	120
To My Mother by Linda Benninghoff	131
My Hands by Linda Benninghoff	132
Rain by Linda Benninghoff	133
Allotment by Diana Gittins	134
Beethoven by Diana Gittins	135
Losing Her by Cathy Whittaker	136
Kill Me Pills by Cathy Whittaker	137
A Better Life by Cassandra Passarelli	138
Lighthouse by Bill Trüb	146
Nové by Bill Trüb	147
Bazaar by Bill Trüb	148
Williamette by Bill Trüb	149
Parklife by Kenneth Paul Stephen	150
Contributors	157

Glimmer
Tonya Mitchell

One night you will be sitting on the couch waiting for your mother to get home when your world will fall apart. The cocoon that is your life will split open and you will think, *This can't be happening. This can't be real.* You don't know it yet, but years from now you will press your forehead to a windowpane, brush your cheek against a gossamer memory, and think back to this night. For now, plant your feet on the floor. Sit up straight in your pink elephant pajamas and look from your mother to Walter. Wait for the words, all of them, because they are the only things keeping you in the room.

Your mother is breathless, flushed. Hands flutter to pearls—your father's pearls—at her throat. Her painted eyelids flicker like twin butterflies the color of indigo. She is wearing a new dress in her favorite color: aquamarine. A shimmering chiffon you helped her pick out the last time you went shopping together—an event you now see—just this very minute—as duplicitous. Perhaps there is a change in you for Walter, who stands beside your mother, steps back a pace. As if it suddenly occurs to him that this should be a private conversation. Among family. Mother to daughter. But don't look at him, look at your mother. Sit up straight in your pink elephant pajamas. Resist the urge to crumble in on yourself because now you know. You *know*. Wish that she would speak to you in her native German so that you could reply back honestly, cruelly, *Ist dieses ein Witz? Is this a joke?*

But it is English words that cascade from your mother's mouth soft and intimate as rose petals. Crimson blooms of joy straight from her heart. They float to you on a hidden current propelled by her enthusiasm but when they reach you, they transform into needles. A thousand little needles—biting, sharp and purposeful. They stab at you, pierce your flesh like an army of fire ants. Breathe them in, each and every prickly word, feel their burning descent until they come to rest in the pit of your stomach. Commit them to memory. File them under T, Things to Mull Over Later, when you are alone and can breathe:

In love
Surprise
Proposed
Getting married
Happy happy happy

Break your rule and look at Walter whose eyes are an apology. *It's okay,* they say. *I know this is a shock.* Don't stare at his thinning hair, his creepy, towering frame. Instead murmur nice things. Hug your mother. Try not to flinch as you shake Walter's hand. Ask to be excused.

Sit on the edge of your bed. Try to imagine your room the way it was before the news. When the chair was just a chair, the pile of shoes in the closet just a pile of shoes. Now every object in your room seems tainted, complicit in the conspiracy that has become your life. Walk in circles. Bite your thumbnail down to the quick and ignore the dull throb. It is nothing compared to the pain of your mother's betrayal. Pretend none of this matters, that you are the same person you were yesterday, five minutes ago, before your mother came home and the bottom dropped out of your life, but you know it isn't true. Scream silently to the world how unfair this is and tick off the reasons why: (1) You're a good daughter and you don't deserve this. (2) You and your mother are doing just fine alone thank you very much. (3) Daddy, God rest his soul, wouldn't like this.

Imagine yourself packing a suitcase and shimmying down a drainpipe. Try on future daring roles for yourself. Teenage runaway. Hitchhiker. Thief. Juvenile delinquent. Turn off the light, crawl beneath covers and have a one-sided conversation with your father. *Daddy, I don't like him. Daddy, he's not you. Daddy, what do I do?* There is no reply. Later, when you hear your mother's step on the stair and your door opens, pretend you are asleep.

You walk beside your mother with your head downcast, wind whipping knots into your hair you will later regret. Brown sugar sand oozes between your toes as seawater pools at your ankles then slides away, a motion that always leaves you slightly disoriented, no matter how many times you experience it. A yellow pail dangles from your hand filled with the morning's harvest of shells, starfish, the occasional fragment of sea glass (oh, the prized sea glass!). Your mother stops to poke a lump with a stick and uncovers the remains of a jellyfish. She straightens and moves on, an aquamarine blur on the edge of your vision. A short distance away your father lies belly-up on a faded beach towel, a hat perched on top of his face. Despite days of unbroken sunshine and shirtless sunbathing he remains ridiculously, comically pale. Your mother turns to you, mischief in her blue-green eyes, and the two of you approach with stealth. You overturn the contents of your bucket onto your father's torso and dash away. Your father sits up gasping, sputtering, flailing—making the most of this moment, this pearl of a moment. He makes a run for you and you shriek, tearing down the beach as fast as your spindly seven-year-old legs can carry you. Look back and he's chasing your mother whom he scoops up and carries into the surf. Wind-whipped laughter reaches you in waves. Take it in, savor details: Your mother's long, tanned legs, your father's smile as they tumble in the water, the kiss he plants on her before they submerge, lips still locked.

Remember, too, other things about those two perfect weeks in Maine: your first taste of lobster, buttery smooth and silky in your mouth; a catamaran adventure that left you green and lurching; midnight campfires on the beach that made your sunburn ache; the caressing glances your parents gave one another when they thought you weren't looking. Don't remember, *forget forget forget* that that sea—the sea you laughed in, the sea you worshipped—is the same sea that claimed your father weeks later when his plane went down somewhere over the Atlantic.

Weeks pass and you do not know your mother. Ever since the announcement that she will marry Walter, she moves as if under water: unhurried, graceful, languid. She touches your shoulder, your cheek, your arm, for no reason at all—while setting a plate in front of you, passing you in the hallway. Your mother hovers two inches off the ground. Clearly, the weight of your hopelessness can't keep her there. You want your mother back, the mother who fretted over bills and laundry. You want to argue about chores and homework and boys and curfews again. Be clever. Don't blow it. Disguise your fury behind a mask of reserved delight. Tell her how happy you are for her and Walter. Never let on how much you hate the way she pronounces his name in her staccato German: *Valter*. Don't tell her how much you despise his hunched-over gawkiness, his balding head. Instead, make a plan and file it under H, How to Undo What Has Been Done. Wait for the opportunity and when it presents itself one night at dinner in the form of an offer—Walter's offer—to pick you up that night after a late school football game, smile and accept.

Hours later, when the game is over and the crowd is dispersing into the parking lot, wave goodbye to your friends. Step into Walter's car. Watch raindrops quiver and streak across your passenger window as houses blur past. Steal a look at Walter bent over the steering wheel. Watch his profile turn from yellow to red to green beneath the glow of a traffic light. When his car pulls away and hisses into the night, don't look back. Meet your mother at the door. Fall into her. Breathe in her scent and fit your mouth around ugly, jagged words:

Touched
Scared
Pressed
Hands
Walter Walter

Watch your mother unravel. See the maelstrom of emotions flicker across her face: shock, disbelief, anger, revulsion. Her eyes and fingers move over you. *Hast du Schmerzen? Are you hurt?* Reassure her. Tell her of your narrow escape. Feel yourself gathered to her—fiercely, protectively, hopelessly—as she murmurs promises into your hair.

Press your face into the soft curve of her neck, a perfect place to hide a smile.

Fast forward forty years to a hospital room. Each time you enter it, fear is a cold fist around your heart. It is the way your mother lays there—eyes closed, hands folded, skin the color of ash—as if already prepared for eternal rest. Your heart ices up but you step closer anyway, see the gentle rise and fall of her chest and relax. Each day you practice taking deep yoga breaths at her bedside because it is the only thing that keeps you composed enough to repeat the ritual again another day.

The name for this place, *hospice,* is a slithery whisper, a serpent on your tongue. You despise the word, the hopelessness of it. Sad resignation permeates the walls that even the nurses, with their bright scrubs and perky greetings cannot mask. Even so, you welcome their pretense at cheer. It breaks up the monotony of the empty hours, the morbid inevitabilities. You lack the courage to ask them, *Excuse me, but can you help me find the strength to watch my mother die?* Your attempt at keeping yourself from falling apart manifests itself in the performance of rituals you believe your mother would appreciate: arranging fresh flowers on the table by the window, massaging her hands, playing Bach's *Brandenburg concertos,* her favorite, on a CD player next to the bed. You speak to her of her grandchildren, of the weather, until you can no longer stand the sound of your own voice. You have memorized the water spots on the ceiling along with the repeat pattern of lilacs on the wallpaper. Each day, you follow the cracks on the floor as if they might lead somewhere different. The doctors remind you—as if you might forget—that it won't be long now. She will not regain consciousness. The mammograms and biopsies and chemo treatments have all culminated into these last days. The machines tethered to your mother are not there to prolong her life but to draw attention to its conclusion. It is the way she wanted it. Your mother may still draw breath beside you, but she is already gone.

Grab hold of your mother's hand and try to squeeze life into her fingers. Ask yourself, *Who is the old woman laying there?* Do you recognize the sunken valleys of her cheeks, the deep fissures of her forehead that the ravages of pain and illness and age have left behind? Wonder when she got so old. Calculate where the years went. Take your mind on a journey through your years at university, your career as a history teacher at the college, your marriage, the birth of your two daughters—now adults themselves. A sequence of events that made your mother proud. Remind yourself that they were your years, not hers. It is not that she didn't take part in your life all those decades—she did—it is just that she remained on the periphery. There but not there. A presence that seemed to gradually recede—with her silences, her isolating retreat into German—until the mother you'd once known was no longer there.

Rise from the chair beside your mother's bed and walk to

the window. Outside, dusk is quickly surrendering to night. The last of autumn's leaves, dry as bones, skitter across the parking lot. A cluster of off-duty nurses disperses to their cars, headed home to loved ones oblivious to the horror of words like *terminal, malignant, coma.* Press your forehead to the glass and close your eyes. Let another memory into the room. The smell of your mother's attic, the dust that danced in the light streaming through a window. Feel again the old and familiar prick of needles deep within you when you'd pulled an aquamarine dress from a box, sifted its filminess through your fingers, brushed it against your cheek. You were surprised she kept it after all these years. Your mother never spoke of Walter after that night he'd brought you home. Crouched and filthy on your mother's attic floor, a vision came to you: your mother standing before you flushed with happiness. Brimming with joy. Walter watching your reaction as you'd taken in the news. You'd wadded that dress into a ball and thrust it back into the box so quickly you'd almost missed the packet of letters at the bottom. The rubber band that bound them together came away in pieces at your touch, freeing five envelopes addressed to your mother in a man's clumsy hand.

Dearest Helga, I cannot imagine your horror over what you think I have done, but since you told me you never want to see me again, I must resort to this letter...

Dearest Helga, I must try again to set this right and make you see that nothing inappropriate happened between me and your daughter...

Dearest Helga, I've received no response from you, but I must let you know how much I miss you...

Dearest Helga, I love you. I cannot live without you. This is agony...

Dearest Helga, if I do not get a reply to this letter, you will never hear from me again...

Turn from the window and step to your mother's bed. Tell yourself you did the right thing all those years ago. Tell yourself he wasn't for her, that her life was complete. Say it again and again and again until the light grows purple outside. Until shadows creep over bedrails and cover your mother like a shroud.

Shield your eyes from sunlight winking off the casket. Ignore the headache you feel coming on. Cling to your husband's arm because your heels are sinking into the not-quite-frozen ground beside your mother's grave. Around you the small band of mourners is breaking up. The service is concluded. Thank God because you cannot look at your mother's grave, the heaps of white roses, the perfectly rectangular void in the ground any longer. Your husband and daughters form a protective arc around you as friends approach, kiss your cheek, murmur platitudes and retreat to the warmth of their cars. Your husband leans in and whispers he and your daughters will meet you at the car. They'll just give you a moment with your mother. Smile and look away. Fight the sudden urge to laugh loudly and hysterically.

Stand there alone and squinting in the cold November light. Ignore the pounding at your temples and wait for words. Try to summon tears. In a few moments you will leave your mother so that men you do not know can lower her into the ground—and you cannot cry. Your soul has departed. What remains is the ache within. The prick of a thousand needles.

Turn and see a man a full head taller than the others making his way towards the cars. He walks with a cane, with the calculated deliberateness of the elderly. Keep walking. Say to yourself, *It cannot be.* Look away and back again. He is still there, moving away from you, his back rounded with the years, his hair gone. But there is no mistaking that frame, those long limbs. Walk faster. Curse the mud. Ignore the pain in your head, the thudding in your chest. Faster, faster. Stop and gulp air against a headstone. Ignore the sunlight that stabs at your eyes. Start running. He is disappearing through the trees. For just a moment—a glimmer of a moment—you see an aquamarine blur beside him and then they are gone.

David Underdown

3 a.m.

Those nights when sleep leaves you stranded,
a sand-bound hulk on the bed
of a long gone sea.

Heavy-lidded, flannel-headed,
straining for familiar sounds,
a scutter of rain, the riffle of wind.

Outside, over Cumbrae
distant house lights blink and tremble,
dance through drifting veils.
Inside a silent presence of machines,
garnet in the dark,
an amber eye on the skirting.

Unkempt thoughts,
their tangled skeins,
searching loose ends
among the wind-snagged rigging.

To sink and watch
the hulls of passing ships,
keeled and barnacled.

And later, a wandering absence of light
against the star-pinned dark.

7.10 a.m. Friday 16 October 2009

Outside the morning is arrayed like an experiment
as if someone has split it into parts
to find out what it's for:
earth and sky are taut as rubber bands
stretched to just before they snap,
dark matter prism-ed from fire to infra-red.

Rolling back behind my head
a caul of cloud;
in front the still impenetrable shore;
and in between a slit of light
as if the furnace lid has been prised up
to yield a glimpse into the heart of things.

Trapped in the gash of sky, an early gull.
The wind-farm waves its arms in miniature
and sixty miles away that smudge must be the Pentlands.

I could fall
into the promise of this morning,
ride its rush across continents.

Fathers and Sons

The tall man whose back I watch stands strong
on his centre ground, on his own now
though the curl at the nape of his neck
still touches me; and somewhere in the distance
is the careless rapture of tossing him skywards,
the space between my waiting hands as he falls back
squealing delight in the danger,
when he was smaller and I was stronger.

Behind, an old man is lost for words
about the present choosing instead
to mind when we built dams of sand,
creating reservoirs where water rose and held
while we fought hard to mend each breach
before it broke and flooded down the beach.

Lichens

It's not far from the grave of my third born,
half an hour at most
back through the cemetery gate,
up the brae to the turn of the track
and the line of steadings along the line of the hill;
yet, for me, half a lifetime now
to that time when I first found
how life could fail on you.

Some journey that,
just when I might have thought
another glitch was sorted:
the evening at the hospital
like TV when you want to change channels.
And next morning to realise.

Last time at the grave:
the stone has given purchase
to lichens that texture its grained surface
but make the writing difficult to read.

While we slept

they must have dragged themselves
along dark channels rutting mud
their swollen bodies carving grooves
through cool ooze. Leathered skin forced apart
tight marsh grasses and clumps of fern
to find high jinks and kerfuffle
under the moonless sky,
the slop and tickle of pond-play
in a thick broth of spring slime
where lovers were waiting to swell to the rhythm
that insists this is the time.

He would have waited, beadily,
an old pro with nothing left to prove,
confident his call would be answered,
that there would be takers for his mottled sack
stuffed with gene juice
and randy again for the next round of the old game.
Last night must have been a threesome at least,
mounting and being mounted.
Spawn slithered implausibly
from its small distended source.
Seed spurted blindly in the blind dark,
foam boiled over into jellied mounds
as the cup flowed, on and on.

And this morning we marvel
at the sheer volume of the stuff
piled there amongst the reeds
like left-over tapioca
but each bubble pregnant with a wriggling pupil
primed to do it all again.

Null
Viccy Adams

Although the sleeves have been rolled back on themselves three or four times, the arms of the shirt are still too long, too loose. They knock against the glass of whisky and disturb the piles of paper she is trying to arrange on the rug. She pushes at them impatiently, focussing on the titles of the records stacked in no apparent order up against the wall. She pushes the sleeves up past her elbows, one after the other. Then she crooks her arms, catching the falling material in the crease. As she brings her arms, wrists turned upwards, hands loose, against her chest, she rocks back on her heels, and takes in the sweep of the wall in one look. Brown, dusty, dimly lit. Patches on the wall where things have been for a long time, been marked in place by tobacco smoke, then been moved. An empty space on the far end of the shelf where the whisky bottles had been kept, stocked, stored for a rainy day. Outside, through the unlined brown, dusty curtains, the sky is light and hard.

She hadn't been here for years. Not since he'd first moved in. How long had she been visiting for then, an afternoon, a week? The memory feels vague yet familiar, but only really because she had already known all the furniture from other places he'd been, other spaces he'd lived in. She remembers the phone call when he bought it, his first and only step on the property ladder. She came down on the train and, yes, stayed for two nights. Maybe three. On the couch. Now she has been here for ten days, sleeping on fresh sheets in an old bed. The first couple of nights were cold and restless. Then she found the dusty brown rugs on top of a wardrobe. Now she sleeps like a drowning mind; she gives up and lets it all wash over her and then wakes up, tired but able to function. The sleep feels good. It lets her feel useful, at peace. It's what they've all been telling her to do; rest, sleep, let it sink into you. She eases herself backwards, lying down on the rug, sleeves spilling down her arms again, and shuts her eyes.

What had her friends said? Cry. Come On Paula. Let It All Out. She hadn't been able to tell them that she wanted to hold it all in, Remember every last detail. Grasp onto every last emotion with desperate, slipping hands. Take every breath as if it could build a wall between her and the world. The world which just kept on turning, kept on moving forward, moving on. Keep herself from forgetting anything. Keep herself from letting go and losing herself in that tide of numbness. The fear that she wouldn't feel anything at all, ever again. Here, in this apartment, there is so much still to be done. There are a lot of reasons to get out of the old bed every morning. The bottles of whisky help her to find her way to sleep when she gets tired.

Her legs, clean and pale, are getting cold. She sits up again and tucks them in underneath her, pulling the edges of the boxers as close to her knees as possible. The glass of whisky is half full, half empty. She hasn't tried this one yet. Highland Park, twelve years old. The end of a bottle, possibly left over from that trip to Orkney. She remembers him going. He loved Scotland. The photos were all the same, him in front of some patchy grass and some grey stones. The only interesting thing about the series of pictures were the ever changing women. Fat, thin, blonde, brunette. Some of them were named, some of them remained enigmas. She guessed they had remained enigmas to her brother too. There are no traces of them here, just the photos which she'd brought with her and then left on the table in the hallway, not wanting to bring back anything that didn't belong here anymore. That had been another thing which they'd stopped talking about these last few years. Apart from the photographs she would have been unsurprised to hear he'd been gay. Or asexual. She hadn't known him well enough to be shocked by any revelations. She had, she supposed, lost her preconceptions. Did that mean she'd stopped caring?

The mysteries of the record system click into place. Of course. There is no system. They're just in piles. His favourites would be the ones on the top of the piles. The ones with greasy marks round the edge of the paper covers. Pleased, she picks one at random (of course. At random. How else would he have done it?) and lets herself listen. It sounds like the first taste of whisky; spicy, horrible. Too much. Then it kicks in and warms her from inside, brings her back to life. One more step towards working it out. Because there has to be a reason. There has to be something in this place that will help her understand what happened. The list is growing.

This is what he wears
This is what he drinks
This is what he washes his hair with
This is what he cooks
And now, without doubt, this is what he listens to.

Jazz, of course. She doesn't recognise any of the names. But that doesn't matter. She'll learn them, in time. The books come next. There will probably be autobiographies of musicians. She hasn't looked, yet. She can piece together the ones he really, really loved. The ones with broken spines. The ones with, maybe, annotations. Or ticket stubs buried in the pages. Then she can learn what the music would have meant for him.

In the meantime she stands up, sleeve drooping almost into the glass of whisky. The clock says dinner time. She isn't hungry. Hunger went first. It would be good to be hungry again. To feel need and desire. She has made herself keep eating since it happened, mechanical, instinctual. Sensible. Tonight she decides to wait for a while, give her stomach a chance to feel its own sense of loss. Glass of whisky, three quarters empty, a quarter full. She walks, unsteady feet, into the hall and retrieves her mobile from her handbag. When the flat phone stops ringing and switches to answer-phone, she mouths along with his words. She has almost perfected the inflection. Rising at the end of 'sorry', falling and maintaining the lowness of 'back to you'. Instead of the beep, she allows herself a whoop of satisfaction, feeling the vibrations of the noise coursing through her veins.

When they were teenagers, he hadn't been into music much. Not that she can remember anyhow. He'd played the guitar for a bit. All the boys she'd known had. She can't remember if he was any good. There are a lot of records, all along the wall. No wonder this place is so dusty, she thinks. No wonder with all his clutter. So much to be sorted through. So much to learn about. When they were younger than teenagers, back on the cusp of memory, she remembers spending hours repeating everything he said. Word for word. Following him round the house, muttering it under her breath. She remembers him getting angry, thinking she was teasing him. And her bewilderment. She'd idolised him, for a bit. Her mother had always reminded her of that phase. The perfect older brother. She'd lied for him, covered for him, helped him, worshiped him. If he'd been into a band, a genre, she would've been into it too. She would've remembered, shared memory. Shared experience. Lived experience. Back when they lived under the same roof, ate the same food, breathed the same air.

Her mouth tastes sour. She walks through to the bathroom, tiles cold and pale against her bare feet. His slippers are far too big. She'd tried shuffling round in them, but they kept falling off. She'd tried layer of socks, paper balled into the toes. It still didn't work. They just didn't fit, plain and simple. His toothbrush is old. The last day or so it has begun to leave bristles in her mouth. And they will run out of toothpaste soon. She could get hers from the bag in the hallway, but it isn't the right brand. She will have to write it down, make a list for when she next has the energy to go to the shop on the corner. Or would he pick things like that up in town? She'll have to go to the corner shop first, check what it does and doesn't stock. Puzzle it out from there. The door on the bathroom cabinet is a mirror, but the wrong face stares back at her. Inside the cabinet is the usual junk of razors, plasters, bottles of pills. No prescription medication. The autopsy said that there was nothing in his system. Not even anti-depressants. Just as well, all things considered. Sometimes the days could be too long. Maybe she should try and eat something now.

The kitchen catches the evening sun and, under different circumstances, would look lovely. The fridge is, suddenly and surprisingly, empty of food. How long is it since she went outside? The deepening colour of the light in the room catches the empty whisky bottles; mimics the colour of the liquid left in her glass. One last mouthful. All gone. Everything all gone. She has eaten all his food. She has drunk all his drink. How does she feel? She feels bored. She is bored of the dirt in his flat, bored of his oversized clothes getting in her way, bored of the damn music. At least she can do something about the music. Pulling the record off, it leaves a deep and gratifying scratch all the way across the surface. This one is ruined forever. She wishes he'd owned a TV. She puts the scratched record on top of its sleeve, then puts them back on the top of the pile. Then back to the kitchen to stare at the empty whisky bottles. Try to work out what he did when he got bored.

Sue Moules

On The Night of a Full Moon

This is a spell to make things right:
plant when the moon is waxing,
harvest when the moon is waning.
The eyes of the cat are copper circles,
its feline body sussurates
along the cold pavement.
As I name the stars and planets,
call on their wisdom,
the continuity of sky,
the crunch of autumn leaves on grass,
short days and dark nights,

Short days and dark nights,
crunch of autumn leaves on grass,
the continuity of sky.
Call on their wisdom
as I named the stars and planets.
Along the cold pavement
its feline body sussurates,
the eyes of the cat are copper circles.
Harvest when the moon is waning,
plant when the moon is waxing.
This is a spell to make things right.

Marina Sanchez

On Seeing a Framed Paper Nautilus
Argonauta Argo

Light rippling through
the two frail shells,
this unchambered vessel
still whole,
after its journey
from ocean to shore.

This glinting on the glass
and I'm back watching
her in the incubator after she was born
after she was taken

from me, how I
waited and waited
for my voice to rise up
through dark water
to hear it ask,
Can I hold her?

View

It takes years
just to sit on a bench,
in autumn,
trees tipped with topaz,
vermillion berries,
grass flattened by dew,
October birdsong,
late butterflies on the breeze,
the flash of emerald across the blue.

Marion Ashton

The Hide at Minsmere

Last light on the last day
of the year, the low realms of sky
an unlikely sequence of horizontal stripes—

indigo, turquoise, magenta—down
to where the sinking sun spreads
red ink across the furthest reed-pool.

Midnight will be difficult. Five of us,
not six, this year. What to say.
Still unthinkable that he could leave.

Within the hide's ritual hush,
lenses point and move in unison, slaves
to the marsh-harrier's every breath—

held glide, dip, rise, loop and dive.
I watch you, friend of forty years,
lost in the bird, your features slackened

into sadness. On the marsh, the hawk flickers
to ground, and if he rises one more time
it will be too dark for us to see.

The Halt
Jane Draycott

On the platform of the small station the woman stands, hands on hips, facing into the sun, staring down the tracks among the brambles into the distance. The young man watches her from the opposite platform.

She has been standing like that for five minutes now, not moving except for her white hair just caught by the breeze. She has no bag, nothing. As if she's just stepped out of her back door to come and stand there. Just the two of them. The music on his earphones is like a soundtrack and the woman is the centre of the scene.

The station consists of two short platforms and a footbridge with a push-button information speaker which has never worked all the times he's tried it. This year someone has replanted the old flower tubs and rose beds and painted the edging stones white. Like some old person's garden, or a miniature railway in a theme-park. He thinks, you go through a war or a lifetime of working nine to five, maybe driving a lorry or a nurse in a hospital working all hours, and what does it add up to—just years of quietly planting flowerbeds and painting the edging stones white. He takes off his earphones and listens to the rails ticking in the heat.

He puts his rucksack down on the bench and sits down beside it like a companion. He can hear the bees, working among the blue spikes of the flowers. The woman hasn't moved at all, at least he doesn't think so. As he unwraps the sandwiches his mother has made, he feels the metal seat burn through to his thighs and considers crossing the footbridge to eat at least one sandwich in the shade over there—there's a single seat in the shade of the dark, high bramble bushes. But the place has fallen so still and the woman so motionless that he doesn't like to disturb the quiet.

So he stands in the full sun and takes a bite. Here on the platform the cheese so familiar from the fridge at home tastes all wrong, sweaty and alien, like food brought home from on holiday. He feels sad for his parents in a way he has never done before.

The woman turns and starts to pace up and down the same bit of the platform, to and fro, back and forth with her arms folded and her head down. Like someone trying to make a decision, or waiting for a phone to ring. He watches her as he eats: her sunglasses look too big for her face and her clothes seem one size too large, as if she's wearing someone else's things.

He's arrived so many times on that platform, on freezing nights coming home from school all those years and now from university, and always his mother or father there to meet him. When he first went to Bradley they took him in the car and he tried not to cry in the back. His mother claimed she wasn't crying but she was. Then when he was sixteen they asked if he'd be all right getting the train at half-term because his mother would be in hospital for her 'small operation'. He arrived that night in a hailstorm which had started just before the train pulled in. He could barely stand up in it, and had to stop several times with his hands over his head against the onslaught of the stones. By the time he got across the footbridge it had stopped, but his face and hands felt stung and bruised. As the taxi drove away through a wild fall of leaves he felt he'd been somehow touched by a different, parallel world. A world very close where things were violent and sudden and hailstones were thrown down at you viciously and spitefully from above, with no warning. Like driving away from a play or a film.

The woman emits what sounds like a long sigh, like the hot air catching its breath. She has flipped opened her mobile phone and is dialling with her thumbs. Compared to his mother she seems nimble and fast.

She shouts into the phone, staring hard down the track: 'There's nothing here David, ' and begins tearing at the yellow flowers beside her. 'At the station… The railway station… I am calm,' her voice is like a child's, petulant. 'I am calm but there's nobody here. Why did you send me here? David? '

She throws her chin up at the sky and then with a great shuddering sigh she is down on her hands and knees wailing. He wishes now that his parents had stayed and waited with him, but he'd insisted they go. He can't see what has happened to the woman's phone; perhaps she is kneeling on it. He looks back towards the car park in case someone else might be coming for the train.

The woman is crying more quietly now, lightly rocking on all fours, her sunglasses on the ground between her hands. There is definitely no-one except the two of them and he knows he should cross the footbridge to help her. He could help her up at least. He thinks about how soon his train is due and whether to take his back-pack. He tries to check the time but his phone is impossible to read in the sun.

When he looks up he can see she's calmed down a little and is sitting back on her haunches, gazing down the in the direction he himself will soon be heading. She is looking at the dusty tree-lined road up to his flat, the corner shop where'll buy some beer, the concrete courtyard where his friends are probably already sitting drinking, his empty bedroom in the afternoon sun. Is she expecting something to arrive from there for her?

There are things in that direction of the tracks that his parents know nothing about and never will, like the December night he nearly drowned jumping from the bridge with Dom and James, the river paralysingly cold and unexpectedly fast. Or the afternoon he lost his virginity with the headmaster's daughter on the same sofa they had all sat on for the prefects' Christmas party. Or last month's meeting with his tutor and the news that he'll probably fail this year unless he can work some kind of miracle with his dissertation. Are spatial memories strengthened in the human hippocampus during slow-wave sleep? It is hard to work out why he chose this title or why anybody thinks the question is important.

'David! David!' The woman is trying to get up, shouting down the track, right up close to the platform edge.

Now he is running, vaulting up the stairs of the footbridge, across the echoing metal gangway and down the other side: she is on all fours again like a dog. As he bends to offer her his hand she looks up at him. Her face is smoother, much younger than he'd expected and her reddened eyes are a startling ice-blue. She looks frightened of him for a second and then some realisation dawns on her.

'Alex!' the woman says his name, surprised only as much as if she's opened the door and he's arrived earlier than expected. He recognises her. She used to have brown hair but he knows it is her: David Olivant's mother. The sun presses hard down on both of them, his black t-shirt soaking it in like a firebox though her hand on his arm is cold. He cannot believe her white hair.

'Dr Olivant—' he wonders immediately if he's got it wrong.

She looks up at him and a wavering smile transforms her face, 'Little Alex. I never thought you'd turn out so tall. What happened in the end with your knee?'

'Oh that's fine now.' Actually it isn't, it was one of the things that had slowed him down in the river. "But I just wondered—are you all right?'

He helps her up—she feels astonishingly weightless and bony. At primary school David Olivant's mother was different to the other mothers. She was confusing because she was also Dr Olivant. When he had pleurisy and his father took him to see her, there were pictures of David on her surgery wall. David was smiling and wearing a jumper Alex had never seen before. He realised at that moment that Dr Olivant knew nothing about the kind of boy David really was. The way he told lies all the time to get other people into trouble. The way he'd stolen Alex's idea for the summer play and claimed it as his own. That day in the surgery none of them knew that David would hang himself in the garage in Year 11. How could they have done? His father had told him the news that same half-term of the hailstorm and his mother's operation. They were in the kitchen and his father was heating up tinned chicken soup, with his mother pale and almost unrecognisable in bed upstairs.

'Are you feeling alright?' Alex asks again. But Dr Olivant says nothing. She puts her hands on her hips again as if she is about to take on a mob or a whole village and stares down the rail-tracks into the sun. A hot breeze funnels down through the station. Alex smells the roses in the white-stone flowerbeds and thinks of that afternoon on the headmaster's sofa and how after it was all over she asked him what A levels he was taking, then told him that he needed to put his shirt in the laundry before chapel. He didn't know if she meant it was her perfume, or him, his smell. He is mortified now to suddenly remember it so clearly.

The rails begin to click, coming to life like some animal woken. Alex looks across at his backpack still sitting on the blazing hot bench. Dr Olivant seems calm again, stock still and staring at a point somewhere just below the horizon. He sees her phone under the yellow bush and offers it to her.

'I'm sorry, I've got to go,' he says. She shakes her head in irritation. He recognises the movement now from the time he had to walk home with them from the schools gala and David refused to stop doing air-swimming as they walked. She has her hand to her mouth now and is whimpering slightly: a light has appeared above the shimmer of the rails, far down the track at vanishing point.

He turns and looks into the distance in the opposite direction for his own train, but the long space back is empty. 'Are you waiting for the train?' he asks.

'I don't know,' she wails. 'I don't think so. What do you think?' Her face as she looks at him now is nothing like Dr Olivant's. She looks like a terrible refugee, her mouth open and shapeless. He notices the ice-blue flowers on her blouse, the same blue as her eyes, and her tiny diamond earrings.

A small white car has drawn up in the car park and a man whom Alex thinks he has maybe seen before is walking slowly down the opposite platform, past his sitting backpack and on towards the footbridge. His body is seized in a strained kind of stiffness, his gaze set straight ahead. Even in the heat he is wearing a jumper. When he gets to the middle of the overhead gangway he stops and stares at Dr Olivant and then waves. She doesn't wave back but turns again to gaze down the track.

As the light of the train grows closer, Alex stands beside her. Behind them he can hear the bees working ceaselessly in the blue spiked flowers. He realises that what he thought was the scent of roses is actually coming from the small yellow flowers right beside them. He looks across at the rose beds opposite, the pale flowerheads just coming into bloom. Someone comes and does whatever it takes to keep them like that, fresh and weeded, someone who cares enough about how people waiting at a station might feel.

Sharon Black

Fathoms

I sit on the jetty
casting my net into silence
directly below my feet,
later into pools.

Hours pass; a tug:
the water opens like a flower's
petals scattering
and I'm yanking light.

There it is: a bright blue word,
thrashing its silver belly,
the thick set of its mouth
turning over and over.

How beautiful it is:
how blue — the colour of eyes,
of a sky, uninterrupted,
although on closer inspection I see

it is in fact a tongue
deprived of oxygen, quivering.

*

A doctor presses a wooden spatula
into my mouth.
Aahhh I obey
and whole seas spill out.

His expression is serious.
There are islands queuing
at the back of my throat,

several miles of reef

and a raft-load of sailors
in soiled clothes,
half-starved,
who haven't seen a woman in weeks.

In a nearby cove, humpbacks surface
like phrases.
The sailors haven't seen them yet
but have struck

upon a coconut tree
and a freshwater source.

*

The doctor's frown
is a familiar scribble
as he replaces his spectacles
and hands me the prescription.

It is crisp as salt crust,
his writing like seaweed,
his signature
a tangle of net.

I nod like a goby behind thick glass,
sift white sand, begin.

After Skye
b. 1999

And you were born at that moment:
beneath Storr's peak you grew
raw as the bay,
its mist, its crocheted shawls.

I felt you in my bones
as the sea air salted my tongue,
your seed bedding down
like a word.

Your name on my lips
was the sting of whisky,
my grandfather's moustache,
blackberries scrumped at the farms of Mearns.

A wind was brewing,
the sea shedding its pelt
on the flesh-coloured sand
before cutting its feet on the rocks.

Eight years on you break my own waves,
shiny from sweat, vernix, brine;
the tiny squall of your body
fighting up my belly, mouth wide open,

rooting for the island of my breast.

My Parents' Bedroom

They slept in an ocean liner,
a padded, studded headboard
at the bow. Straight
across the hall from mine,
it gleamed like royalty.

Over there, my mother's dressing table:
white, gilt-edged,
a glass sheet over damask lace
on which hairbrush, comb and hand mirror
nestled in velvet.

Here, my father's crumpled handkerchiefs,
a scatter of battered paperbacks,
bridge magazines,
the soft balls of yesterday's socks:
a trove of sweat and grime.

Evenings he would return,
raise the anchor,
draw curtains over the portholes
and tell us tales
of the strange new worlds he'd seen.

Alone, I'd creep
across the purple pile,
hold my balance against the sea's sway
and drape myself in silks,
pearls and white high-heels.

Slipping in on Sunday mornings
between the salty air and deep skin,
I'd lie awake listening
for the creak of beams and planks
and the scuttling of galley rats.

Onset

Everything is as it was yesterday:
the blurred moon of her face in the mirror,
hair still slurred from sleep,

her hands folding cold water
as her lenses slide into place,
sun splashed across porcelain.

In her hand the toothpaste,
cap unscrewed, the pearl of its head
striped through with red.

She looks at the brushes
splayed like flowers in their pot
and hesitates.

Her synapses snap to red alert
to test for chinks, rewind the thread,
but it's drifted like a sky-coloured bird.

She remembers her grandfather's barber shop,
the striped pole twisting in the sun
—like humbugs, he'd said

his rheumy eyes squinting—
in his confusion he'd even asked
for a poke of pear-drops instead of a hair-cut

before being helped to his seat
as her twelve-year-old self
swivelled with embarrassment.

She weighs the ballast of her stomach
and picks the pink;
its bristles are rough, too rough on her tongue

so she pushes them to the back of her mouth
fixing on the mirror, fixing
on the froth over-spilling her lips.

Flutter

I want to capture that little bird,
the one from my dream
in which a cat stalks
tenement rooftops all night
sniffing out uncaged thoughts
in their nests.

I want to capture that little bird
and perch it in my kitchen
so I can admire it over breakfast
so I can place crusts and prayers
at its neat, silvery feet
like a shrine.

Bridget Thomasin

The Way Back

A strange road
shaping
the space between
river and rock.

The known way gone
frozen footprints
lost in sudden thaw.

The white scent
of winter
hides familiar landmarks

violets
by a broken fence
a hollow tree
the warmth of wild
strawberries.

A tangle of birdsong
empties the night
following threads
of darkness
into the past

beyond the bend
in the lane
the shadow across
the road
shielding the place

where the first slow
flakes fall and settle
snow to cover the dark.

Soup
Jane McLaughlin

The pan is warming on a low heat.

He watches her as slowly and precisely she cuts the onion in half with a sharp knife and then turns the two half-globes face down and slices them finely, exactly along their latitudes, the white crescents falling on to the chopping board.

'White rainbows,' he says.

In the last six months he has begun to see and say things she would not have expected before.

Then she lines up the lacy white slivers and turning the knife the other way, chops them into tiny pale dice. She peels the lilac and silver skin from four cloves of garlic and slices them thinly into little discs.

Now she pours a golden stream of olive oil into a measuring cup and tips it into the warmed pan.

She picks up the chopping board and sweeps the onion and garlic into the oil. She turns up the heat a little and begins to move them around with a wooden spatula. The mingled smell of onion and garlic begins to rise into the room.

It is a bright autumn morning. The kitchen is an extension built on to the house and has windows on three sides, letting in the autumn sunlight. There is a garden, bright with the colours of autumn leaves.

It is an expensively simple kitchen, built of slate and plain fitted wood, with a mixture of modern and antique utensils around the worktops and walls. It looks like a kitchen modelled on one from a previous era, perhaps her mother's.

A man of about thirty-five sits at the kitchen table. He is quite tall, casually dressed. His hair is a light reddish brown. On the left side of his head most of the hair is missing, the ear is crumpled and the skin of the side of his face is badly scarred.

The woman looks about the same age or slightly younger. She has the same hair and brown eyes. She scrapes the skin from four carrots and begins to cut them into orange discs, flat and even.

'Last time you did the celery first.'

She looks at him again.

'Yes, I did.' She does not say: 'You remembered.' She says: 'Have you seen Dr Hanson this week?'

'Yes, I went on Tuesday.'

'Did he say anything new?'

'Nothing new. He says it will take a long time but I am doing OK.'

'Just keep taking the tablets?'

'He didn't actually say that. But yes, that's what it is.'

The bright patch of sun from the window has moved round to where he is sitting. He seems to respond to the warmth and brightness and shifts his chair a little to get more of them.

Now she takes two sticks of celery. In one movement she cuts off the base, slightly brown and earthy, and neatly pulls the strings out of the back of each stick. Then she turns them lengthways on the chopping board and slices them. They follow the carrots into the mix in the pan. Then two sturdy parsnips, a turnip tinged with lilac, some chopped tomatoes and passata.

'She didn't make this soup very often, but it was one of our favourites. I can remember coming home from school on the days she made it—there was the smell of minestrone as soon as you came through the door. Great on a cold day—I used to put my fingers round the bowl and thaw them out. Then sticking my spoon into that thick hot liquid and tasting—tasting all those things but not separately, all blended and melded into the wonderful Italian taste.'

Cauliflower florets, some chopped potatoes, some thinly sliced courgettes are added to the pan as she talks.

'She had an Italian friend—Vittoria, her name was. From Genoa. She had come here in the sixties as an au pair and married an Englishman. Nice couple, he did something in scientific instruments. And she was the most amazing cook. Mum tried quite a few of her recipes, but the only one she ever really felt confident with was the minestrone. '

'What did Vittoria think of it?'

The woman laughs. 'To be honest, I can't remember. She may have given it her seal of approval. But so what, we loved it! That great pot sitting on the stove, Mum spooning great bowls of it out when we came back from school, and then some more when Dad came home... And there used to be such a performance about getting the vegetables. We all had to troop off to the allotment in the dead of winter to dig up parsnips and pull the celery. I used to hate it—I'd much rather have been at home in front of the fire but of course there was no way we were allowed to. But he was so proud of the things he grew, and to be honest, I've never tasted better celery. We'd have it for tea, lovely cold crunchy celery'.

None of this is true.

'I like growing things.'

'Yes, they do quite a lot of gardening at the Centre, don't they? Do you get any vegetables?'

'We'll probably have some cabbages soon. 'Didn't we get cabbages from our neighbour at Merefield?'

'Mr Tomaszewski? Yes, I think I did mention that. Well, when he was in a good mood. But more often he was throwing stones at the dog or making sure we did not walk on his grass.'

Three kinds of beans—cannellini, borlotti and kidney have been boiled separately and mixed together, and then poured into the mixture. Finally everything is in and the pan bubbles slightly at a low rolling boil.

'Right,' she says. 'Shall we go?'

They walk out into the brightness of the morning, along a street where orange leaves are piled in the gutters, and then down a footpath that opens on to a wide common bounded by woods on all sides and scattered with clumps of bushes and brambles.

There are a few people about, the odd dog walker, a couple of joggers, legs dutifully moving in time to whatever music they can hear in their headphones.

In the far corner is a football pitch where two teams of schoolboys chase a ball, their shouts faint across the grass. These seem to catch his attention and as they walk he follows the progress of the game.

They come to a point where the footpaths cross.

'Which way do you want to go?' she asks.

'That way,' he says, pointing to the left. 'I remember we went to the right last time, up to the woods.'

He has never been along the right hand path to the woods. They walk for an hour or so, skirting the woods and then following a different path back through the shopping centre and some more autumn tinged roads similar to her own. He talks little, but she keeps going with her series of anecdotes and stories from their childhood, of family and friends and neighbours.

He stops and says: 'I can remember a field like this. I used to go there with boys from my school. There was an old donkey in a paddock and he used to look over the fence at us and make the most awful noise. I remember that a boy—I can't remember his name—fell in the ditch full of water. He was afraid to go home with his school clothes all muddy and wet. So he came round to our house and dried everything out in front of the fire. I think he got into trouble anyway.'

She laughs. She knows it is not true.

Perhaps he has begun to understand.

They stop to buy a paper and then turn back to her house. As they walk along she takes his arm. He seems to be tiring. His step is sometimes a little hesitant, not exactly a limp but a slight hitch as he brings the left leg forward.

As they open the door and walk through, the scent of the soup floats out to them: rich, garlicky, warm.

'Well, some things are just like home,' she says.

She puts two bowls and two soup spoons on the table. The sun has moved round and comes now only through the western window.

She ladles soup into the two bowls, thick, hot, its ingredients visible but smoothly enveloped in the thick juice of tomato and vegetables.

They sit, eating the soup in large slow spoonfuls.

And as she eats it, she tastes all the bitterness of old betrayals and grief. Of a mother who left when she was five years old and before that never made them so much as a bowl of chips. She tastes a father who got through a bottle of vodka before breakfast and after that had no idea who he was hitting or why.

For years she and her brother lived in the grip of this madness. There were aunts, friends, people who gave them clothes and food when they needed it, but no one who was brave enough to make sure that they were taken from him. Their time at home was mostly nothing. No TV, no books or music, no friends or visitors, sometimes no heating, light or food. It is the great stretches of unstructured nothingness that she remembers most. These were punctuated by storms of violence, but once these had passed nothingness took control again. It was not until they were old enough to tell their own story that they were believed and taken away.

She eats slowly, trying to overcome the revulsion she feels at the sliminess of the beans, the glutinous liquid in which these dead things float.

She runs upstairs to the bathroom and is violently sick. She spews up all the vegetables and seasonings she has so carefully prepared, spitting them furiously into the lavatory and then pulling the flush. She sits for a minute on the bathroom stool. She feels purged, clean.

When she comes back he is still placidly spooning his way through the soup.

He looks at her.

'Are you OK?'

'Yes, of course. I just needed to go to the loo rather suddenly.'

'Ah all right, I thought there must be something wrong.'

'No, everything's fine. The soup is great. Even better than last week. It's really reviving, somehow there's nothing like good soup for building you up.'

She smiles.

She does not want to remember. She does not want him to remember. Why should he want to remember lying in the darkness in a chaos of broken glass and body parts, losing most of his own blood, and, as it turned out, all the life he had lived before that day.

He is lucky that he cannot remember. He has a blank screen on which only what he chooses can be written. And what she chooses. His loss is her gift. In the space that was emptied out by fire and darkness that morning she can put the life they never had.

And is this such a terrible thing to do? The good times he had with the woman he loved were gone. They died with her in the darkness of the tunnel and he forgot even her name. He knows that she existed, but has no story for her. At some point perhaps some doctor or therapist will take it upon himself to tell her brother that he should work through this, and come to terms with his lost past. Coming to terms—she has always thought it an inhuman idea, suggesting that you can write some kind of contract or agreement with the demons in your life, a contract that will somehow bind them to good behaviour. She is taking nothing from him by protecting him from grief.

'Do you want any more?'

'No. That was great, but very filling. It's set me up for the day.'

'That's good.'

He gets up and takes his outdoor jacket from a chair.

'Thanks for the soup. And the stories. You are a good storyteller.'

'They are memories!'

'Memories then. You are a good memory-teller.'

She looks at him for a few moments. Then says: 'You'll come next week then? Will you be OK until then?'

'Yes, I'll be all right.'

'Well let me know if you need anything.'

'I will.'

She watches him walk down the path and turn into the road. How would he begin to say what he needs?

She goes back into her house and through to the kitchen. She stands for a long time at the window, gazing into the garden, tears falling silently down her face.

Then she goes to her shelf of cookery books, opens one and lays it on the table. She takes a large bowl from the cupboard, scales and measuring spoons.

She puts butter and sugar into the bowl, and steadily, rhythmically, starts to beat them.

Graham High
Road Edge Poem

The animal
  has come apart from itself
where the wilderness
  crops up short at its containment,
where the straight route has cut
  through the entangled wood.
Set type; flat as a template
  and all articulation arrested.
Feet that held to the road
  in the sudden headlight are now
rigidly oblique to the touch of tarmac.
  The moon with its embezzled light
reveals her – a creature all
  spelled out. The vowels of entrails;
the consonants of teeth and claws;
  small syllables of bone
burst out under pressure:
  A meaning of sorts.

Martin Willitts, Jr
Snowy Day
After '*The Snowy Day*" by Jack Ezra Keats

The brownstones are in a white-out
listening to the clock-radio's alphabetical school closings.
I am zipped into two snowsuits.
My mother will not release me into the arctic day without them.
There are gatherings of snow hunched on the low branches
like white pigeons frozen on brick ledges.
I drag a stick behind me in the solemn snow leaving a comet trail.
A snowflake melts on my tongue like a Eucharist.
Stuck cars grind their wheels, madly.
I pack my morning tight into a snowball.
In a blizzard, silence takes over, the row houses evaporate.
There is comfort in hearing my crunching boots.
The damage of the storm is done.
Nothing is moving in the barren landscape except me.
I print my name on a frosted window pane.
I nibble on an icicle shaped like a carrot.
There is nothing in this white world that is not mine.

The snow hesitates, stales, stops in mid-breath
like my grandfather climbing ten flights of stairs.
I drag a sled of quiet to my doorstep.
I unzip my day, leaving a puddle of boots.
Snowplows skate through the ice age like mastodons.
My mother rubs the blueness and tingling
from my fingers, dipping them into water.
She scolds me in a voice letting me know she is half-serious.
It was a collage of things that could have gone wrong.

My day is ending in a blanket I pretend is a snow cave.
Things are happening outside without me.
A child can only do so many things. One is imagining.
The world is shaking its low branches of last snow.
Tomorrow is an open school.

Letter from Chopin to George Sands, 1847

The delicate touch you felt on your neck
is the same as on a piano, with the same lyrical rush,
the music of leaves in the resolute winds.
It is the same idiomatic language of geese leaving.
My heart has the same feeling, restless, yearning.
When I play a rondo, no one can hear the silence after.
I leave these early movements behind
like I must leave you.
Some things are finished when they are finished.

I thought of returning to you.
I hesitated at your window.
I knew if you saw me with that melodic look you have,
it would enrapture me.
Our bodies would become counterpoints.
But it would be fragmentary motifs. Textural nuances
of what used to be.

Our love was illicit, some say.
I say, it was melodic, rhythmic, and full of music.
Our love was repetitions of a single note.

You criticized me for my primitive sense of form
when we would lie in bed, soaked in harmonic intonations.
You were right about me as well as everything else.
I cannot help being in the soundscape of textures,
in the lightness of sound, in the last moment leaving you.
For life is opening one door and descending unknown stairs.

Letter from George Sand to 'beloved little corpse'
Name for Chopin due to his numerous sicknesses

You could not stand a woman who did not act like a woman
except in bed. Even then you were horrified
by the idea a woman could enjoy passion.
What were all those compositions of love-soaked music then?

You were not my first lover and you will not be my last.
A woman should pick and choose who will enter her bedroom.

You shake your head, expecting me to fall for your music like others.

A woman cannot be a slave to men.
You will not allow us to be equal.
So what choice do I have?
What choice does any woman have?

I changed my name so I could publish what scandalizes you.
Women have a right to sincere love and I will write about it.
I shall write about my desires and disappointments.
I will not miss you. I will only find another.

What have you done recently?

Will Kemp

Night Boat

Nothing happened, though
something was happening to me,
as that wake cut the stillness
below the moon, a film of cloud
over the sky's pewter blue.

I sat in a deckchair, alone,
neither lonely or cold,
looking back, the neat trees
and fields of Holland
now a pencil line above the sea,

clear as the week before—
my first drink, Mrs Wouters'
laugh at her husband's jokes,
her worry I'd be sick, my face red
with thinking she was so pretty.

And I am there now,
with that same disbelief
a night could be this light,
a place so calm, and already
the feeling of wanting to go back.

Kesteven

Slung low across
the blue glow of sun-drained light

a dark score of telephone wires
pegged with starlings

which now burst
to pepper the sky in flight

The startled deer

She bolted from the brake,
a rush of brown over the road
and into the winter sun.

I stopped in time
to see the velvet head,
black flecks on her back and stilted legs,
as she eased to a tip-toe trot,
then vaulted the ditch and hedge.

In a moment she was gone.

Though that outstretched leap,
long and clear, stayed
suspended in mid-air.
The way she landed too,
light and soft, already moving off
towards the cover of the woods.

And now everywhere
that forest hush,
when men with spears,
moving through light-streamed dark,
must have first paused
by pale green dots of ash or elm,

and felt the need to capture
those *n*-shaped leaps
on the limestone walls of caves.

This Ride Goes Backwards
Rachel Crowther

Once, when she was a little girl, Ruth went on a fairground ride with a curious sign at the entrance: *'warning: this ride goes backwards in the middle'*. She has no memory of the ride itself, just the sign and the extra dread and excitement it provoked, on top of the usual seasick sense of anticipation, as she and her father edged forwards in the queue.

The memory made its way into her dreams and simmered there until she couldn't be sure whether the ride was real, or whether it only ever existed in her imagination. The dream is more elaborate nowadays – as an adult, Ruth is inclined to question the ride operator (backwards for how long? at what speed?) – but the apprehension is the same, and the surprise, new each time, of being warned about something so unremarkable for a fairground, but also so unnatural. Humans expect to keep moving forward, Ruth surmised. Even as a child she'd grasped that.

It's the day the gardeners come, and Ruth is standing in her kitchen, looking out onto the driveway. She's not waiting for them to arrive, exactly, but she's aware, as she mulls over last night's dream, that the battered four-by-four will pull in soon, and Marie-Claude will spring out of the driver's seat, and Leila, the resting actress, will slide more leisurely, more gracefully, out of the other side.

Ruth was taken aback the first time they came. The name she'd picked up on the phone was Claude, and there'd been enough leeway in the timbre of Marie-Claude's accent to take her for a man. She felt a flash of guilt, that morning, about hiring gardeners: if these women could do it, why shouldn't she? But they were so cheery, and so grateful to have the work. Why should she feel better paying a man to mow her lawn? Now, the idea of feminine solidarity gives her pleasure. They are more than competent, these two. They cherish the garden, exclaiming over the scent of the lavender; in summer, they've been known to garden in their bikinis.

There's a flash of silver outside, a roar as the car mounts the slope of the drive. Ruth shuts her eyes quickly to banish the lingering image of the fairground. It's years since the dream really frightened her; its power is different now, she realises. It comes to taunt her for not taking proper notice of it. She never thought about how unequivocal the wording was: not 'this ride *might* go backwards', but a definite statement. A certainty of reversal, in the middle of things. How had she not grasped that?

The gardeners don't usually come to the door, but somehow Ruth isn't surprised when the bell rings. They are beaming, the pair of them. Ruth's eyes take in the pashminas already half off their shoulders, ready for work; sometimes, waving goodbye at the end of the morning, she sees a flail of colour as they are flung back on.

'We have good news,' says Marie-Claude. 'Leila has a part.'

'Oh!' Ruth's instant fear that she will lose them must show in her face, because Marie-Claude clucks her tongue.

'Not me: only Leila. I will still come. It will be OK for the garden.'

'It's only a few months,' says Leila. 'A short run.' She doesn't have a French accent; Ruth isn't sure whether they're sisters or friends. She has never asked.

'Well, but it might lead to something more.' Marie-Claude shrugs, smiles again. In the pause, Ruth notices the blossom coming out, behind them, on the tree that screens the house from the road, the new leaves darkening already towards the reddish brilliance of summer. 'So, we must get on. Get ahead, eh?'

I have some news too, Ruth thinks of saying, but she has never confided in them before. Nor have they, for that matter. That's been part of the pleasure, Ruth realises, the lightness of their acquaintance, and the way it centres on the garden. Root and branch, she thinks, although she doesn't know what she means by it, and then: I didn't ask what part she's got.

Ruth has to go out this morning. This is something that happens when life goes into reverse: its routines, the taken-for-granted ease of the daily round, are disrupted. Effort is required, suddenly; an unfamiliar grappling with momentum.

She might, perhaps, disguise this in the remains of the old life—put on the dishwasher and hang out the washing, sift through the pile of bills—but now she knows all this is a front,

Ruth can't be bothered. For a while she wanders from room to room, glimpsing the gardeners through the windows (how carefree, she thinks, to wheel a barrow across the lawn!). But being in the house feels too awkward, this morning. Being alone, she was going to say, but the point is she's not alone, any more. She knows what's there: she doesn't want to meet it in a doorway, or notice its impression on her side of the bed.

Half an hour before she needs to, she snatches up her bag and slams the door behind her. Anyone seeing her nosing out of the drive would take her assertiveness for self-confidence.

She's kept waiting, of course. Not just that half hour but an extra one; too long to sustain an impression of sangfroid. This is another thing Ruth has found: the chunks of time that life breaks up into are the wrong size, these days. She's always too early or too late, rushed through things or given too long to dwell on them. The world might look the same from the outside, but nothing fits together any more.

All of this, the distortions and deceptions of life, occupies her so fully that she doesn't hear her name being called the first time.

'Mrs Briggs?' The smart woman is standing in front of her now, a smile hoisted briefly to conceal impatience and a dash of pity.

Ruth follows her down a corridor and into a room with too much light in it. Transactions like this, she thinks, should take place in respectful gloom. Dickens would know how to handle them. The smart woman speaks slowly and carefully, but Ruth can't concentrate on what she's being told. Driving home, she can only think of the blossom in front of her house, the shy pink of the flowers that only last a few weeks before scattering across the drive.

The gardeners have gone, leaving a green sack of weeds and grass-cuttings by the gate. Marie-Claude has left a note, too, pinned to the front door.

Dear Ruth, We started the beds on the right and next week I will finish them. I think we don't need to mow the lawn again for two weeks. I am sorry to inform you the tree by the road is deceased. My friend who is a tree expert has come today and confirmed it. I don't know if you want to do something about it. A bientot, Marie-Claude

Ruth reads the note twice, hoping for something more the

second time.

Then she looks up at the blossom tree with its leaves newly unfurled, its petals intact still. There aren't any other trees by the road; there's no room for doubt. And why, she wonders, should she expect the diagnosis to be obvious from the outside? She of all people should know that appearances count for nothing. It's a fairytale, this hopeful show of new life. It's Cinderella's ballgown, ready to turn to dust at midnight.

Even so, she feels a grief she knows is out of proportion to this particular tragedy. Nature has let her down (has even the spring become shifty and unreliable?) and so, obscurely, have Marie-Claude and Leila. What did they see that she didn't? What else have they been hiding from her, in those green sacks of cuttings and trimmings?

Ruth goes into the house and shuts the door, deciding that she won't come out again. Not for a long time, anyway. She'll face out the spectres that lurk among the furniture. But she takes to prowling the garden in the evenings, when the shadows of next door's hornbeams overhang the lawn, and watching the blossom tree obsessively for the first sign of blight.

Inside, washing collects in corners and bills pile up, along with a sequence of envelopes with the same postmark. Ruth ignores them all. She has been preparing all her life for a siege, she realises: her cupboards are full, evidence of a life-long lack of need. She veers, now, between caution and self-indulgence. One day she makes a whole trifle and eats the cream off the top, like a child. The silver balls crunch between her teeth before she swallows them.

Next time the gardeners come—just one gardener, now—Ruth stays inside, but she leaves a note on the shed for Marie-Claude.
 Should I have the tree cut down? Can your friend advise?

Before she leaves, Marie-Claude posts a reply under the front door, as though she knows Ruth has been there all the time.
 I don't think it's necessary, but if you prefer I will ask him. It's quite common, I think, this condition. M-C

That evening Ruth tours the garden again, wondering which of the other trees are dead too. This little flowering cherry, perhaps, planted the year they moved in? The old sycamore in the far corner? There is a perverse sense—satisfaction, even—in the idea that she has been living all this time surrounded by dead wood.

She leaves another note for Marie-Claude.
If it's really dead, I would prefer to cut it down before it falls.

She has stopped answering the phone, but sometimes familiar voices echo through the house, followed by the bleep of the answerphone. Like ghosts, they sound more pregnant with emotion than they should. When the machine is full the phone rings on, petulant and persistent, until she unplugs it. There is nothing, Ruth thinks, that she can't stop if she tries hard enough. If she leans all her weight against the backwards momentum of life it will grind to a halt, eventually.

Did she go on the ride in the end, she wonders one morning? Did she have a choice?

That day, or one close to it, the doorbell rings, and after a few moments someone knocks loudly on the door: more a drum rhythm than a hammering, meant to rouse interest as well as attention.

Through the study window Ruth can see a young woman. She watches her for a few minutes, listens for a repeat of the rat-a-tat-a-tat-tat. Curious, she thinks, that the girl should be so insistent. There is something about her Ruth recognises: not her features, but an air of detachment, of not-caring, that elicits an answering twinge in her own chest. It might be a warning, but if it is she chooses to ignore it. In any case, the visitor is certainly not a solicitor.

'I knew you were in,' the girl says. She is perhaps nineteen or twenty, incongruously dressed for a warm spring day in an old-fashioned duffel coat and woollen hat. 'I saw you looking at me.'

Ruth shrugs. 'You have to be careful.'

The girl laughs. 'Round here?' Her gesture takes in the size of the houses, the carefully tended front gardens.

'Especially round here.' Ruth means to sound severe, but doesn't. She's prepared to be entertained by this encounter, she decides. Careful is the last thing she means to be.

'So can I come in?'

'What is it you want?' Ruth asks, but she has already opened the door.

'I'm selling stuff.' The girl brandishes a grubby bag, the kind Ruth's sons used to carry their sports kit in. She grins, a sudden rictus, as though someone has told her to smile when she's making a sale. 'I'm Avril, by the way.' She fumbles in her pocket, apparently looking for an identification card, but soon gives up.

'What kind of stuff?'

Avril shrugs. She pulls off her hat, releasing a stream of purple hair. 'People don't usually ask to see it. They usually hand over a tenner and I'm off. You got something cooking?'

'No,' says Ruth, but she turns her head towards the kitchen, just in case the oven has turned itself on in time for lunch.

'I could help you, then. I got an NVQ in cookery. Part of it, anyway.'

Ruth is down to tins, but Avril isn't fazed. She rifles through the cupboards and takes out chopped tomatoes, anchovies, black olives.

'This is a great one they taught us,' she says. 'Got some foreign name. Mix it all up and put it on pasta. You got a tin opener?'

When she's got the sauce bubbling, Avril looks around the kitchen.

'I'd'a thought you'd have a cleaner,' she says, 'living in a place like this.'

'I had a Czech girl.' It occurs to Ruth that she won't have to attempt the pronunciation of Zdenka's name ever again. The thought provides enough impetus to finish the sentence. 'She ran off with my husband three weeks ago.'

Avril looks at her gravely. Her face is plumper than you'd expect, still childlike despite the piercings, the little tattoo of a snake on her neck. 'So you need a new cleaner, then.'

The pasta is good. Avril removes her duffel coat, revealing an assortment of black garments of different lengths, and they eat lunch with stagey ceremony in the dining room. Ruth lights the candles in the middle of the table.

'So,' Avril says, when she has cleaned every remnant of sauce from the plate with her knife, and then her finger. 'You got any children?'

'Long gone.' Ruth's sons, already well into adulthood by their mid-twenties, ring very early in the morning or very late at night from Hong Kong and Los Angeles.

'Living here on your own, then?'

'For the moment.'

'Planning to move?'

'Absolutely not.' Ruth thinks of the stack of vellum envelopes, the bank accounts she has shut down. It was her money, after all.

'Getting someone else in, then? A bloke?'

Taken by surprise, Ruth laughs. 'I hardly think so. I'm nearly sixty.'

Avril shrugs. 'My Gran's seventy, been married four times,' she says. 'What are you going to do, then? oulder away here eating baked beans?'

'Moulder' is what catches Ruth's interest. More than the NVQ, it suggests an education. A brain. The both of them, she thinks, wasting their lives.

'What happened to your course?' she asks.

Avril frowns, as if this is more personal than the questions she's been asking. 'I had a baby. Gave it up.'

'The NVQ?'

'The baby. Had it adopted.' She shrugs again. 'Give it a chance,' she says. 'Her.'

'That must have been hard.'

'Yeah, well.'

There is silence for a moment. Ruth, who has become so used to silence, finds herself jittery. Tinned peaches, she thinks. There were some left in the cupboard after the trifle. But she can see tinned peaches isn't what Avril needs.

'You could stay here for a bit,' she hears herself saying. 'Help me clear up the house. Do some cooking.'

The party is Avril's idea. Ruth is supposed to ask some friends too, but although the comic potential of a mix and match guest-list is tempting she can't think of anyone she wants to see, except the gardeners.

They order the food on the internet. Avril is no keener than Ruth on going out, now she's found her way here—and why bother, when someone will deliver? They order clothes for Avril too, then clothes for Ruth. Ruth demurs, but Avril insists. For the party, she says. She chooses flowing things and tight things, not designed to go together, that make Ruth look like a naiad. Ruth twirls in front of the long mirror in her bedroom and can't help smiling.

Sometimes at night she hears Avril downstairs, opening cupboards. At other times, Ruth wanders around the house while Avril sleeps, wondering which of her possessions she would miss, and what her family would think of her open-door party invitation. She considers locking the silver away but doesn't.

'You got a lot of books,' says Avril one day, when they are moving things around, rolling up rugs and cramming spare furniture into the study.

'My husband was a bookseller.'

'Oh.'

'Antiquarian books,' says Ruth. 'Second hand,' she adds, with satisfaction.

'A lot of money in that, is there?'

'Not as much as there was. He gave it up last year. Moped around at home, after that.'

Ruth stops, one hand on the back of a sofa, and contemplates the bookshelves, rows and rows of spines lined up like dead things in a museum.

If she'd cleaned the house herself, Zdenka would never have been here.

If she'd looked after the garden herself, would she have noticed that the tree (which has held its blossom longer than ever this year) was in decline?

Avril's snake tattoo curves and recoils when she shakes her head. 'Spilt milk,' she says.

The funny thing, Ruth thinks, is that she can contemplate most of the spilt milk with equanimity. She has fewer regrets than she expected, than the smart lady solicitor tallied up for her. What troubles her most is that she misjudged Zdenka, and is obliged now to hate her. She set too much store by the girl's patience with her inept pronunciation.

Avril's culinary range has turned out to be limited, but she is good at re-heating. *Let Waitrose make entertaining easy*, say the slogans on the packets. There's a lot of alcohol too, mostly of a type Ruth hasn't seen before. Small bottles of brightly coloured liquid fill the sideboard in the dining room, wedding-present tumblers lined up beside them.

On the afternoon of the party they make a trifle.

'Beautiful,' says Avril, and it is. The huge glass bowl is the perfect shape to show off the different layers. Like coloured sand in the Isle of Wight souvenir that sat for years on the kitchen mantelpiece, Ruth thinks. She is tempted to delve into the cream, but she knows Avril would be shocked.

By six o'clock they have laid out all the food on plates and oven trays. The kitchen looks like Aladdin's cave.

'Do you think anyone will come?' Ruth asks.

'Course,' says Avril.

And they do. Ruth expects them to be late, the young people who are Avril's friends, but the bell starts to ring at seven thirty. Most of them look sceptical when the door is opened, some of them suspicious, but they perk up when they see Avril.

'Hey,' she says.

'Hey,' they reply, perhaps with a flicker of a smile, and they amble across the hall in a docile line, like schoolchildren on a museum visit. Ruth looks out for the ones Avril has mentioned: Billy with the green crewcut, who was at college with her until his Mum had a relapse; Toni who's bringing her guitar.

The cocktail sausages go first, a hundred and twenty of them, cooked with mustard and honey.

'Very nice,' says the boy who takes the last one, peering regretfully into the empty dish.

When someone lights up Ruth rushes round with makeshift ash trays. She realises too late that they might take her eagerness for anxiety about damage to her furniture. She smiles, adjusting her flimsy turquoise neckline, to show she's perfectly relaxed.

'OK?' she asks. 'Having a nice time?'

A young man comes to find her in the kitchen while she's rescuing trays of spring rolls from the oven.

'A bit brown,' she says, batting away steam. 'Oh well.'

'You must be Ruth.' Ruth notices, as he shakes her hand, that he's older than the others, careworn rather than bruised by life. 'I'm Mike. I used to work with Avril.'

'Oh?' Ruth scans her mind for a mention of past employment, draws a blank.

'It's very kind, what you're doing.'

'It's fun.' Ruth slides the spring rolls onto a platter edged with pink roses. Hideous, she thinks, but never mind. 'I love parties.'

'Not just the party. Taking Avril in. Giving her your trust.'

'It's been good therapy for me,' Ruth says, reaching for the right language. Her mind is moving too slowly, she realises, missing cues. 'You're a social worker?'

'Probation officer.' He smiles, and Ruth's mind shifts again, coiling and uncoiling like Avril's snake. 'You know she's applied to rejoin her NVQ course?'

Ruth feels a spasm of panic, but Mike's next words quell it.

'Are you really happy for her to stay on here?'

'Of course.' Ruth basks, for a moment, in relief. Of course I am.'

Avril appears in the doorway, and Ruth has the strange feeling that they have been discussing her dowry. She looks like a bride, Ruth thinks, pink-cheeked and happy.

'Someone's asking for you,' Avril says. 'Won't come in until you come to the door.'

Marie-Claude, thinks Ruth. 'Take these,' she says. 'Spring rolls. Very hot.'

But it isn't Marie-Claude, or Leila. Standing in the doorway, paler and smaller than Ruth remembers, is Zdenka.

'Rooth.' Her inflection draws out the vowel into something soft and beautiful. 'Oh, Rooth.'

'Hello, Zedenkar.'

'I have nowhere else I can go.' Zdenka's eyes are dry, but Ruth doesn't hold that against her. There's no doubting either her timidity or her temerity. The bag she has with her is pitifully small, and even so it's half-empty.

Ruth's heart is beating fast. 'Come in,' she says. She doesn't want to guess at the details of what has happened; the fact that Zdenka is here is enough. Enough of an explanation, and enough for her. 'Come in: we're having a party.'

'You should not forgive me.'

'No use crying over spilt milk,' Ruth says, but she is thinking of other occasions now. Who knows how much was spilled before, at all those book fairs and literary festivals and trade conventions Malcolm was so keen on?

Avril and Zdenka, she thinks. Alpha and Omega.

The doorbell rings early the next morning, before anyone else is awake. There are bodies curled in corners, stretched on sofas, sheltering under tables. Like Battersea Dog's Home, thinks Ruth; more strays than you could hope to find homes for.

This time it is Marie-Claude.

'I came as soon as I realised,' she says.

Ruth smiles. 'I'm afraid it's over,' she says, 'but it's nice of you to come.'

Marie-Claude frowns, glances over her shoulder. 'The tree,' she says. 'Not *deceased, diseased.* I make mistakes still. I am sorry.'

'Diseased,' echoes Ruth.

'It is not so serious. My friend says we should maybe remove one or two branches, but the rest is fine.'

It isn't so much the sparing of the tree that silences Ruth as the restoring of faith. She stares at the blossom until it blurs to a pink haze, pricked by sunshine.

'Come in,' she says, after a moment 'Let me make you some coffee.'

In the kitchen, Marie-Claude sits while Ruth fills the kettle.

'How is Leila's play going?' she asks.

'It's not a play, it's a little part on the television. But it may become a bigger part, she thinks. She is very happy. Perhaps I have to find a new partner, though, for the gardening.'

Ruth glances out of the window as she reaches for the cups. It's a brisk morning, the branches of the tree stirred by the breeze. As she watches, a flurry of petals wafts into the air and drifts down like slow-motion confetti. Out in the hall, there is another stirring, a shifting of bodies and creaking of floorboards, a series of little sounds moving through the rooms around and above her. The house is coming to life, she thinks. Inside, somewhere, she can feel an answering grate of gearwheels, tightening of joints, sighing of cables, as the fairground ride eases itself slowly into forwards motion.

Lynne Taylor

Woman sitting in the sun
A stilled life

The danger
is what she has done
tomorrow.

I stroke her shoulders
with circular motions
under the loose neckline
of her dress,
soothe the burn
that hasn't happened yet.

Reluctantly
her muscles give in:
fingers slide over mine
as she begins to forgive
what will happen
yesterday.

Gavin Goodwin

The Brutalist School

It was a brilliant exposition
of concrete construction, modular design
and orderly planning.
                     The prize-winning structure was
Unloved and derided locally…seen
as a liability…failing
 the area's children.
                     And here we come,
walking the tarmac lane into the grey container,
into the chasm
                 between one
version of the story and another.

Woman at a Window

Swinging from the handles of the pushchair
a polythene bag stretched with tins—
swinging from the handles, cutting at her shins
as she pulls the buggy up
the concrete stair case. Armpits of her blouse
dark with sweat. The bulb in the stairwell
burns a cold yellow light.
The steps smell of urine.

At the window, her back to the kitchen,
her son watching television.
From the window she looks out at the square—
a cherry tree dense with blossom.
She looks hard into it: the clusters
of petals get thicker, softer.
She wonders, if she fell,
would those branches catch her.

Eabhan Ni Shuileabhain

Pretty Woman

It is cold here
in the darkness
beneath my skin.

I have left the moon behind.

I look only
as far as my feet,
as far as my hands.

When I paint my eyes,
I hold the irises
Tight in kohl-black,
Remembering lies.

I try to count my ribs
before breakfast,
before lunch.
before dinner.

Every time I lie down
My eyes leak.

I feel the liquid gathering,
Feel it escaping
To pool in my eardrums,
Wet and strangely cold.

Bilocation

Today, my mother and sister
>went to visit my father's grave.

I stayed away,
my arms still buried
elbow deep in the soil,
my face pressed
into the worm rich grave,
knowing that it is still
Only clay that separates us.
I have yet to believe
that he has journeyed anywhere
>except to that small plot.

And I cannot leave him there.

The Buddha's Footprint
Cassandra Passarelli

The old man hesitated before he stepped from the bus onto solid ground. Clinging onto the window rail, to stop from being ditched into the aisle, he'd doggedly taken in glittering reservoirs, abundant jungle and unspotted sky that lay still, behind glass. They arrived in Dalhousie after dark. He stopped at the first hotel for *kottu* and sweet tea. Refilling his bottle with water he knotted his *lunghi* tight about his waist and followed the trail of stalls selling hats or slabs of sweetmeats. The vendors huddled, drinking tea. He wondered who bought so many scarves and sweets since he appeared to be alone. But as one, and then another, pilgrim overtook him he realised there were many.

Flickering bulbs, curling around the peak's toppled-sand-castle silhouette, lit the way. Behind him a ripe moon filled the sky with preternatural light. This place was sacred; the Yatavara monk who'd sent him was right. Apart from his village, Elkaduwa, he'd never been anywhere else; a couple of miles from home he already felt like a foreigner. A sinewy octogenarian, he'd not spent much time around people. His long matted hair was unwashed, lips and teeth stained with betel and dark skin cracked and dusty. Most remarkable were his large, clawed hands. He'd a wife and children once but they'd left for the next life, or Colombo. Alone in the forest, he cut Vs in the bark of rubber trees, collecting fishy sap that leaked into coconut shells pegged beneath.

Many pilgrims were already stumbling down Sri Pada. Some threw their feet down haphazardly as if drunk on *arrack*. Groups of boys, sporting knit hats or towels against the chill, sang in brash voices. One bounded past, narrowly missing the old man, and tumbled headlong into an old lady in white who fell, rice beneath a scythe. Her withered husband stood dumb over the crumpled heap of her. The rubber collector fumbled in the folds of his *lunghi* and pulled out a clean blue handkerchief. Helping her sit against a step, he tied it around her bleeding elbow. She raised her dark violet-fringed pupils to him in gratitude.

She and her husband had walked the entire way from Wayagama, on Tilak's behalf; Tilak stayed behind to mind the fruit shop. He was a fine boy but he had enough of Wayagama. Since the troubles started, visas to the Middle East were as hard to get as lotus root; someone suggested Peru. Tilak laid hands on a tourist visa in New Delhi's Peruvian Embassy. His mother fell ill, so Tilak held off. But a stray South American backpacker, passing through Wayagama, bought a pawpaw and recommended Lima as a fine city with plenty of work. Tilak made up his mind; it was time.

Part of her knew he was right. The shop was a fragile buffer against chaos but the situation was dire; war, poverty and inflation were rife. If she were a young man, she'd be on the next plane. Tilak was all she had, but she couldn't hold him back. Her husband was a burden, who cared more for his betel, areca nut, lime and tobacco than his arthritic wife and ambitious son. Life with Tilak on the other side of the world was hard to imagine. She would have to sell, buy fruit and keep accounts without him. One day, as she disconsolately washed clothes at the falls, her neighbour told her to take her woes to the Buddha. So she bought herself a white skirt and her husband a white *lunghi* and they set off with a lunch box of rice.

When they started climbing she had second thoughts. She was a strong, wiry woman but her usual exercise was limited to between piles of woodapples and coconuts. After an hour, they appeared no closer to the yellow rectangle of light encircling the giant footprint. Her feet ached, she withdrew into herself. When the boy crashed into her, she raised her arm, saving her face but fracturing her elbow in two places. She shut her eyes and realised her foolishness. She might have been at home, selling satsumas and Chinese apples. Life was in this moment, not next week when Tilak would leave.

When she felt the gentle fingers of the rubber collector on her arm peace filled her as though she had reached the summit and been blessed. When she heard children squeal she opened her eyes.

A haggard man sat on a bench beside the path, his youngest

child curled on his lap. The elder two, undaunted by the climb ahead, leapt and mimicked frogs that echoed in the undergrowth. The little boy cried:

'What's that on your foot?'

'A sleepy worm,' his sister answered.

'Look, *Thanththa*, look, *loku akka* has a worm on her heel!'

Their father peered at the rubbery cylinder coiled about her anklebone.

'A leech.'

'Oh, *Thanththa, Thanththa*, take it away.'

'We need a little lime or salt... wait, I'll get some from that stall.'

'Here,' the old lady pulled a tiny jar from her blouse, 'some *Siddhalepa Balm*.'

Thanththa dabbed ointment at the leech's head. Recoiling, it dropped to the ground, leaving a bright red stream of blood.

'Thanththa, Thanththa, look how red the blood is. Look! Look!'

On the stones, the leech flexed and stretched; a vein with a life of its own. Her father ground it to a pulp with his bare foot.

'Thank you, Madame,' he said passing back the salve, 'very kind. I hope you haven't hurt your arm too badly.' She smiled thinly. 'We lost their mother last year – she always wanted to see the Buddha's footprint; I was busy, never seemed time. But, at last, here we are.'

He rose and the children scrambled after him.

They skipped up the steps, the eldest leapfrogging and croaking ahead. Not long after they stopped to rest once more beside a cluster of stalls. *Thanththa* bought four plump black mangosteens. The children shone the skins on their t-shirts, stripped them of their fleshy leaves and wheel-of-life navels. Tearing away bitter red pith, they popped the sweet white cloves into their mouths and spat out black seeds.

A solitary *aranyavasi bhikkhu* appeared dressed in dark rust robes. The driver stood and bowed as a sign of respect; the forest monk waved him to sit. *Thanththa* offered him his own mangosteen. He accepted with a nod, putting it in his saffron cloth bag. He was handsome, with a square jaw, pronounced nose, soft eyes framed with thick unshaved brows. His skin shone.

*

He came at a steady pace, cloth bag swinging, umbrella in one hand, step firm and sure. Each time his foot touched the ground he smiled inside, thinking of the Buddha. He recalled his mother, who'd visited Sri Pada before he was born, and his brother, who climbed this path before his death.

'Have you come far?' asked the father.

'From Anuradhapura.'

'The sacred city.'

'Yes, I live in the Lankaramaya temple.'

'Is it your first visit to Sri Pada?'

'Fourth. And you?'

'First. My wife wanted to come... she died last year. I've come for her.'

'I am sorry for your loss. The world is full of suffering.'

'And you, do you suffer?'

'I lost a brother in the war and my mother. I miss them.'

'Did you choose to be a monk?'

'Let's say I was encouraged. I come from a good family; we have a doctor, the soldier that was killed and an accountant in the family. It fell to me.'

'Funny... we poor folk think it's just us that don't have choices. I'd rather be a *bhikkhu* than a tuk-tuk driver, but it wasn't my calling.'

'It seems appealing, the ordered life; others' respect, a reserved seat on buses, alms. But the hard work, the discipline, is on the inside. Times are so troubled on our Sacred Isle... ' he lowered his voice. 'But I talk too much. Today we must concentrate on our walk, the same Lord Buddha took two and a half thousand years ago. Let's take each step with the Buddha. As you walk think of your wife. Each step you make, make for her. You'll find great peace. You have three lovely children... bless them all.'

He soon found himself behind a group of city boys in baggy jeans, designer t-shirts and knitted hats with headphones or musical mobiles, reeking of stale cigarettes. They laughed and sang, racing, jostling one and other, occupying the path's breadth. How like his dead brother they were, unfettered and happy. But of course they'd suffer as they grew old. Reluctant to disturb them, he remained a pace behind.

'Look at Siripala,' joked one, 'in such a rush. Wants to get back into Pushpa's arms.'

'Not just her arms,' another chimed.

'Who can blame him? I would run up the peak and back to tuck my face between...' His voice trailed off when he registered the flash of monk's rust robes behind them.

'Go on, say it, we're waiting,' teased the others. The young man, blushing red, turned and stuttered an apology. The monk said what was expected of him:

'Try to keep your thoughts pure.'

The boy hung his head. The monk fished in his bag for the mangosteen. Instead his fingers found his prayer book and, thinking how much more value *sutras* would be to the boy than fruit, handed him the book and strode ahead.

The boys spent the next hour in subdued silence. Heady with exertion and altitude, muscles fluid, they used the metal handrail to pull themselves up the last steep stairs. First light glowed at the horizon and groups of women in white descended, chanting songs for the Buddha. As they reached the summit, they were surprised how packed it was; pilgrims covered steps and walls like snow. The boy recognised a group of students he studied with at Colombo's science faculty. Among them was the girl he loved. He wove through the crowd to get close and squeezed his way between her and her best friend. Just then, gold-rimmed puffs, heralding sunrise, gave way to the sun's oyster pinks and blood-oranges, flanked by monumental stacks of goose-grey clouds. He turned to his love and planted a gentle kiss on her full cheek. She smiled and took his hand in hers.

When the sun rose, they began the climb down. Giddiness, generated by five thousand steps and heightened by tender feelings, made everything radiant; old people, young men, mothers and children glowed. She let go of his hand just once when they stopped to drink water and let the shaking subside in their legs. A small child, in her mother's arms, woke up and began to sob. The girl reached into her denim pocket and pulled out her mascot, a bronze elephant the size of a two-rupee piece. She held it up to the child who eagerly closed her plump fist about it.

A few hours ago she'd never have parted with this treasure.

But now, brimming with love, her heart was open; she had no need of anything but the boy at her side. The weary mother smiled gratefully at the young man, who carried the gurgling infant, and they continued together. Near the last stretch of sellers he put her down; she took her mother's hand and walked.

A *Rammanah* monk, feet planted firmly at the roadside, was offering blessings. He called to them. The mother had only the bus fare home in her blouse, but she couldn't refuse. The monk held the child's wrist in his and pronounced a prayer, wound the orange string twice about it and tied a knot. Then he held her mother's wrist and blessed her. Before she could pull the twenty-rupee note from the folds of her *sari,* her daughter lifted her arm above her head and dropped the bronze elephant into the alms bowl. The monk beamed broadly and her mother sighed with relief.

When the crowed thinned, the monk wrapped the alms in a cloth, placed it in his cloth bag and made his way up toward the monastery. The money would go to repairing the stairs. Some thousand steps up, on the side of the path sat the beggar Keerthi, without feet, polio legs twisted. He'd climbed up on crutches at dawn, as he did every day. The monk lifted the bundle from his bag and wriggled his fingers in amongst the notes. He pulled out sixty rupees, enough for a plate of rice and curry, and gave it to Keerthi who hobbled off at once to the nearest stall to order breakfast and sweet, milky tea.

The stall-holder was in good spirits; he himself was hoping to make a barefoot pilgrimage that very day to Tooth Temple in Kandy, open just one week every six years. The city would be awash with pilgrims in white, waiting patiently in the queue that curled around the lake. Those that couldn't get in would take shelter under the arches and pass the night on the pavement, awaiting first light to take their places once more. His trip was in the balance... he must sell all his rice and curry today or he'd not have the fare. But things looked promising. If the day started with the old vagrant, Keerthi, setting foot in his stall, he was in with a chance.

Philip Madden

End of the day in the wood engraver's studio
#ai suki—woodblock carving knife used for the finest details—

Sometimes he sweeps up like a barber.
Just to get the hell out. Go for a drink.
Sometimes, like a hairdresser.
But still hair.

And then sometimes he sweeps
everything else
before making ai-suki
finishing cuts.

Cups the feather fine curls
in the palm of his thoughts.
Such letting go
as fine as what stays.

He thinks of the fine
hairs on her face.
Thinks of the shedding
of tears and skin.

Halley's Comet Visiting Rights

Once a month. No overnights.
That was hard.
So I missed a few.

And when I came back
the kids were busy or bored.

Each time I returned
I was further away.

So I missed a few more.

Pretty soon it was every 75 years.

Piano from Mars

Listen!
Do not
listen to
the official
story that
this grand
piano being
played by
a Spanish
pianist on
the concrete
concourse of
a run
down block
of flats
in Brussels
is part
of an
Arts Festival
this grand piano being
played as
smoking men
in white
vests and
veiled women
look out
from balconies
is a
butterfly from
Mars blown
off course
by a
solar wind
which heavy
with Earth
is just
getting its
breath and
lightness back.
Listen!

Padraig O'Morain

Achilles in the farmyard

He set down a round of ash
with exact concentric rings,
quickened his mind, swung the axe
and cleft the wood so cleanly the halves
stepped apart like dancers.

He'd rather timber that put up a struggle,
gnarls and knots that refused the steel,
made it glance like a sword off a shield.
Once he fancied himself Achilles
in battle sending heroes to the underworld

as he turned the stubborn wood this way
and that, split off the edges that fell easily,
cutting closer to the implacable core.
The block, gripping the axe, rose up.
He crashed it down in a rage.

He crashed it down again. It would not break.
He tugged until the blade was free,
then kicked the block aside and, fretting,
left the yard, like Achilles
having met a thing that would not yield.

Cut-throat

Sunday tomorrow. The house goes still.
Her father steadies himself at the basin.
Her mother holds a finger to her lips.
The child stares at the razor,
foam like January snow on his face.
They name it a cut-throat
he told her once. She doesn't know why.
He begins. Child and mother hush.
In the yard, calves and donkey fall silent.
He scrapes trails of smooth skin,
rinses blood-pinked foam
off the blade. Job finished.
Her mother holds out the towel. He turns
grinning, once a week clean, innocent
as anything. Yes, her mother says drily
that's the one I married alright.
Then she goes out to get in the turf.
The child hugs her father and breathes in
the benediction of soap and water.
Outside a calf bawls, the donkey calls.
Lightness comes back to the house for now.

Not talking

Since the final fight, details now forgotten,
when pride sealed up their hearts and mouths
they have made their own mute liturgy:
the scraping of a chair announces dinner,
the car engine turning signals Mass.
Today he makes another vow
to renounce their wordless rituals,
drop onto the permafrost of their days
a solitary phrase to skitter across
the hardened ground of their silence
but he is, as usual, afraid
to violate the long silence of the years
with the sacrilege of speech.

The fool's journey

You set off with a blindfold on,
we wove it for you from stories.
Your dog yapping at your heels may mislead you.
Go with your head high, face the horizon.
Follow the dog to where you trip
on a stone, fall into a ditch.
You learn something here, someone laughs at you
then kindly shows you the wrong way out,
you're down on your arse again in the muck.
Someone else tells you the right way out,
you may not trust kind strangers now.

Beyond the hedge, smoke broods over a town.
You hear a shout, glass splintering.
You want to run back to your ditch
but the dog sees you must approach,
steal in fear along a scorched street
peering over your blindfold,
the taste of soot catching your throat.
Seek the oasis in its heart: a pool
where a fish glides smoothly in peace
until the walls of the pool melt,
water sinks into clay, the fish smothers.

Scramble to the fields past a burnt home,
a girl raped then nailed to a door.
She weeps in your mind as you go until
you come to a small stream where you dip
your feet into the tickling water.
You scoop up silver pinkeens
to make you giggle and they thrash
on your soft palm until you let them fall.
Leave the girl in the stream to dissolve
to water, soil, in a billion years rock.
Then: where's the dog that yapped at your heels?
Where is the blindfold we wove from stories?

Bodies in the machine

He must have put in his nights in this chair
in front of the Bakelite wireless and smoked
while nettles clustered in his front porch
like eager visitors denied admission
though a young ash had sprung up brazenly
in his bedroom, waving out the window
even while he snored, here, out for the count.

Do you want to see his bedroom? No?
Well, the bed sags in the middle,
no sheets smelling of the wash, no woman's touch,
his cap, the pattern grimed, waits on the headboard.
In a blotched photograph his parents
worry. They wonder, perhaps, what a tree
is doing in their strange boy's bedroom.

Sit in the chair in front of the radio.
Its fabric, white the day he bought it,
looks brown as a fingernail from nicotine
Surely it can't still work? Turn the knob.
A little shock as music gushes out on long wave,
Jazz from Marseilles to make young men and women
dance until wine smelling mouths collide.

This was where he went while the damp ate the walls
nettles crowded impertinently in the porch
and ogled warm breathings, close kisses,
while he drank Powers whiskey and smoked, eyes closed,
his closest company the cattle in Moore's field,
until he slumped to sleep in Marseilles lulled
by soft bodies embracing in the machine.

Candyfloss and Doughnuts
Kate Brown

They arrived the day we were leaving. Eight caravans, two Land Rovers, three Tranny vans, a prehistoric Morris lorry and a couple of horses.

'Real travellers,' said Sarah very quietly. 'Gypsies.'

Now we knew why the farmer wasn't bothered that we didn't want to pick strawberries anymore. Never mind the adults, I counted sixteen kids, Sarah counted eighteen and Mel wasn't sure if she had seen seventeen or twenty-two. She said the boys kept swapping jumpers to confuse her.

We sat on the back step of our red and white ambulance, watching. We wanted to talk to the travellers, but what we wanted even more was for them to talk to us. We wanted them to say we were real travellers too. Instead they stared at the peace sign on the bonnet of our ambulance and laughed.

Three women passed a grubby baby girl in an even dirtier stripy romper suit back and forth. The baby grinned; a tooth was coming through at the front. She looked like a naughty pirate. I wanted to go and hold her. One of the women put the baby down on the dusty ground to play, but the baby didn't want to play alone, she wanted attention. I'd never heard a kid scream that way before. Or maybe I'd never really listened.

I got up, went inside the ambulance, and shut the door. Even if the ceiling was too low for me to stand up straight, it was better than listening to a noise that cut right through me. I was shaking. I started to pack things up. Three chipped mugs, a frying pan, a tea-pot, a saucepan, a half open packet of spaghetti that nearly spilled all over the floor and a cheese grater that wouldn't stand up straight. I put everything in its place, feeling like that old woman who lived in a shoe. We'd bought our ambulance just three weeks ago. I remembered how much my arms had hurt hanging the curtain rod because I could hardly drive the screws into the wall, and how I'd evicted a whole family of mushrooms when I fixed the leaky window seals. Putting away, thinking, it calmed me down. I shook the last drips of water from the kettle's belly out of the open window, then jammed it down between our jerry can of water and the gas fridge. Snug, not like when Mel had left it on the stove last time, when it shot into the cab as I braked, and gave Sarah a black eye.

Finished, I stood, half stooped, listening to the sounds outside. The baby had stopped screaming. Mel was checking the oil, and Sarah was cleaning the windscreen. The Gypsies hadn't spoken to us, it was time to go.

It was dark when we stopped for diesel. The garage was just closing up and Mel screeched onto the forecourt. We looked round and watched our new curtains swinging a wild can-can back and forth. Mel giggled. I found a pheasant feather on the tarmac and stuck it in the band of my battered top hat. It felt lucky. Things were going well. We'd got a full tank of diesel to get us to the festival. It was the first time we'd been able to afford to fill right up. When we pulled over for the night, I couldn't sleep. Lying there, I kept wondering about whether anyone had died in our ambulance, and who they might have been. It started out quite comforting, then it wasn't anymore. I just wanted to go to sleep and couldn't.

We drove onto the festival site late in the afternoon. The sky was clear apart from one small fluffy white cloud. It hung above the festival as if it had decided it wasn't actually a cloud; that it wanted to be a guiding star instead. I liked the cloud. Maybe it was another good sign?

We parked up, and I took off.

'Jo!' I heard Mel screaming behind me.

'Joanna!' Sarah joined in.

They probably couldn't find the kettle. I'd stashed it back in its safe place after breakfast. I strode on, grinning, wondering how long it would take them.

I held my arms out like an aeroplane and ran down the slope in front of me, yelling at the top of my voice. A few startled weekenders jumped out of my way. A dog-on-string free of its string snapped at my ankles.

The site mechanic raised his crowbar to me in greeting. 'Hey, blue eyes.' I smiled at him. The man had a cushy number. A fiver for each yuppie on mushroom tea that locked his keys in his car.

Over the next rise, I stopped so suddenly I nearly fell over.

There, parked at the centre of a huddle of vehicles, was the pink fire engine. Pink, fluorescent, falling apart and, not meant to be there. I stared at it. Breathed hard, sucking air into my butterfly lungs.

He'd said he was going to Spain.

There was a jewellery stall about a hundred yards away and I set my eyes on it. I tried to walk towards it. If I could get there, I'd be all right, if I could get there, I'd be safe.

I couldn't.

I pictured Jake inside the fire engine. Standing by the wood burner, making tea for all the people who'd be visiting him, 'cos everyone loved Jake. A kettle whistled sharply. I jumped. Someone took the kettle off the stove, laughter rang out. This wasn't fair. I hadn't meant to be right.

I closed my eyes. I don't know why, it was the worst thing I could've done. I imagined Jake. His grubby tailcoat, a little too long in the arm, the elbows shiny from wear. The blue and white striped sailor top, slightly unravelled at the neck, with a rip at the shoulder. Black jeans, almost new, Jake complaining about them, hating to look too neat. Brown leather belt, worn, with a warm and friendly smell, as long as there wasn't too much paraffin in the air. Black work boots, with a big toe poking through in the left foot.

Or was it the right foot?

Shit. I couldn't remember.

The sun was setting. It looked like a giant peach. Down in the valley there was an artificial lake, full of water. Two hours ago, it had been empty. Some people at the water's edge, just coming up on acid, seemed to think this was some kind of natural miracle. I wondered who got to turn the taps on and off. It might not be a bad job.

Bringing coffee and hot doughnuts, Mel and Sarah came and sprawled beside me. I knew they'd seen the fire engine because Mel couldn't keep still. 'Did you see him then, Jo? You said he was in Spain, Jo,' she rattled, waving her arms around. 'Have you given him a 'hello' shag yet?'

I rubbed the sugar on the crust of the doughnut against my lips, bit into the soft warmth. I concentrated on how different a doughnut tasted when it was warm. How exotic.

'Nah. Wasn't there,' I said.

Whoever it was that manned the taps forgot to turn them off. By midnight, the lake was taking over parts of the site. I squelched alone through the mud. The air felt different. A whole horde of clouds dashed across the half moon. I wondered what had happened to the little cloud with the identity crisis.

A track overhung by tall, broad-leafed trees ran alongside the lake on slightly higher ground. I stopped to watch some men juggling, and a unicyclist. It looked like they were just messing about, but then a woman I'd seen before, a tiny Italian with bleached blond hair and charcoal black roots, stepped into the unicyclist's path. A giant shimmering fish was perched on her shoulder. The unicyclist started to ride in circles round her. He glanced over his shoulder at the jugglers, winking, nudging the air. He rolled his eyes, and called out in a building site yell, 'Cor, look at the fish on that!'

The little Italian seemed to grow on the spot. She glared at him, a special glare only a clown knew how to do that made it look like her hair was standing on end. Then she turned and strutted away. Her timing was perfect.

The unicyclist followed and started his catcall again. Holding her fish tight to her chest, the woman turned to him, and in a bitter chocolate drawl, she told him just what she thought.

'A woman needs a man like a fish needs a bicycle.'

The crowd laughed. The woman and the unicyclist prepared to enact a duel.

I moved closer, itching to get a better view, until a familiar gesture, in the distance, stopped me in my tracks. Coming towards me, on the other side of the small crowd, was Jake.

I sprung back and hid behind a tree. I watched as he shouldered his way through to get a look at the show. I studied his face. The crease around his mouth when he smiled, an upside down question mark without the dot. I used to trace it with a wet finger tip. And he'd look at me with his bright green eyes.

I went back to the ambulance. I climbed in under the blankets beside Mel and Sarah, and tried to go to sleep.

In the morning, drizzle flecked the ambulance windscreen. Me,

Mel and Sarah huddled together. I needed to pee.

Mel was lying with her head near to the fridge door. We'd found some alphabet fridge magnets at a car boot sale and she was shifting them round. Sarah and I watched silently as she wrote BANANNA. Sarah reached over and took the extra N out and shifted the letters up. Mel scowled at her.

'What you doing here, Jo?' Sarah asked me sleepily, 'I thought you'd be with Jake.'

I didn't answer.

'Make the most of having her here, Sare, by next year he'll have her up the duff without a paddle and we'll never see her again. She'll be his little wifey.' Mel giggled.

'Not if she sleeps with us, she won't,' said Sarah.

I pulled the blankets tighter round me.

'Well, it's all for the best, then, isn't it?' I snapped.

It stayed quiet for a while, the windows misting up from our waking breath. Sarah looked over at me every now and then. I pretended not to see.

Mel broke the silence. 'Of course, you could say that if he really cared, Jake'd come and find her, wouldn't he?'

'He wouldn't know where to find her, Mel, we only got the ambulance three weeks ago. Remember?' said Sarah, raising her head from her pillow.

Mel sat up and stretched. 'But has he looked? What d'you reckon Jo?'

I threw back the covers, wrenched the ambulance door open and leaped out into the rain in my knickers.

'Pass me that fucking t-shirt, cow.' I pulled clothes on and strode into the woods to piss.

My boots had holes in them. I hadn't taken much notice of this before, but now I was standing at the edge of a shallow puddle, a puddle that got deeper as it stretched out in front of me. On the other side of the puddle, stood the fire engine. Inside, a kettle whistled. This time I counted. One, two, three, four, five... I got to twenty. I walked back to dry land.

Nearby, on a log, sat a beer-bellied hell's angel, sheltering himself under an enormous fishing umbrella. He was eating candyfloss. I liked him immediately for his strange taste in breakfast. I went over and sat beside him. My good feeling had been right; the hell's angel passed me his candyfloss and let me take a bite.

In silence, we contemplated the fire engine and the puddle I would have to cross to get there. When the door swung open, the hell's angel dipped his umbrella ground wards, so I wouldn't be seen.

'Blonde hair, red trousers, white t-shirt.' He paused. 'Male.'

'Not him,' I said.

'Gone now.' The hell's angel lifted the brolley back up again. He had crystal blue eyes.

'Once I loved a woman,' he told me. 'She seemed to love me back; at least I thought so, especially when she gave me a beautiful baby boy. Whenever I was down, she made me happy. However shitty things were, just one look at her made my heart glow. Then one day, I came home early and caught her in bed with another man. He wasn't even a stranger; he was a mate of mine. It turned out she'd been seeing him since the beginning. I didn't know what to do. All my other mates said I should get the baby tested. See if I was really the father and refuse child support if I wasn't.'

The hell's angel passed me the candyfloss. I clutched at the pink spider's web of sugar, not knowing what to do with it and not daring to look at him, let alone speak. But he didn't need me to prompt him.

'I didn't do the test,' he said. 'I still see my son every week, I take him out, we play football in the park. Last week we went to the zoo and saw the new baby giraffe. Me and his mother, we're civil. The same mates who said I should get him tested say it's not fair to keep on seeing him if I might not really be his Dad. So they're not mates anymore, but my boy is, whether he's mine or not.'

The fire engine door swung open again. This time, neither of us moved. A couple stepped out, she had red dreadlocks and he had black.

'Why did you tell me that?' I asked.

The hell's angel stood, slowly. He smiled at me. 'You looked like you were thinking about big things.' And with his umbrella still up, although it was no longer raining, he lumbered off.

Back down at the lake, the water was being drained out. People sat at food stalls, mud up to their ankles, eating veggie breakfasts. I ordered tofu burger, egg and beans. On Monday, the festival would be over, and even if I could hang around for a day or two and help clear up, by Wednesday, I'd be back on the road. Where would I go? I got on with my breakfast and tried not to think about it.

Just as I was forking some beans into my mouth, the plank of wood I was sitting on sagged violently, and another body slid onto it beside me.

I looked up, knowing already.

The upturned question mark, the bright green eyes.

'Hi.' Jake grinned at me.

I lowered my fork and prodded viciously at my beans.

'Hi, Jake.' I didn't grin back. I could practically see the cogs turning in his head as he figured out what to say.

'Did I see you around? I mean, up by the fire-engine. I thought it was you.' He almost managed to sound casual.

I shook my head, hard.

'Oh.'

'No,' I added, just in case he hadn't understood.

I wanted to run away very, very badly, but I had jelly legs. I forced myself to stand up.

Jake took hold of my wrist. Gently.

I wished he'd been rough.

When he spoke, he didn't look at my face, he looked at my belly. I watched his mouth, the way he struggled to get the words out.

'You didn't keep it then?' he asked.

I made myself as tall as I could before I answered. 'Doesn't look like it, does it?'

Jake let go of my wrist.

I didn't see the tree trunk stretched across in front of me, as I charged away. I tripped and fell, flat on my face, in the mud.

Mel and Sarah dropped me off at the top of the lane. I could tell they were offended that I hadn't told them about what had happened with Jake, about me having a bun in the oven then getting rid of it, all without saying a word. It was like I hadn't trusted them or something, and I suppose I hadn't.

Sarah said they'd park up in a lay-by we'd stopped in before, about a mile away. They'd stay until morning, that way, if I changed my mind, I could catch up with them. I said they didn't need to; they should just go on their way. Sarah sat in the cab and cried. Mel pretended to be busy with a map.

I could see the travellers' camp through the brambled hedge halfway down the lane, and the farm a little further on. The prefab office was just closing, but I managed to sign on for a morning shift. I pitched my one-man tent as close to the gypsies as I dared. I had a little gas stove, a milk pan and some tea bags. I started to brew up.

It was getting dark when she came over, the eldest of the three women I'd seen with the baby.

'What you doing here all on your own, love? Where are your mates?' she asked.

She was wearing a bright pink shell suit, so bright it hurt my eyes. She stared at my top hat and frock coat as if I'd landed from another planet. But it was me who was scared of her. My fear didn't stop me following her to her caravan when she invited me in, though. Her name was Karen.

'All gone down the pub,' she told me to explain why there was no-one there. I knew, I'd seen them go.

Karen sat me down and gave me a cup of tea. I told her I liked her curtains and said how I'd struggled to put up mine. She smiled and told me her husband had done theirs. I think she thought it was sad I didn't have a man to hang curtains for me. There was a noise from the bedroom, and she left me in the caravan's tiny sitting room with my cup of tea. She'd put in loads of sugar when I hadn't asked for it. It was quite nice.

When she came back, Karen had the grubby baby from before in her arms. The baby was still wearing the same romper suit, but it was clean. So was the baby.

'My grand-daughter,' Karen told me. She looked too young to be a Gran. I watched her holding the baby. I wanted to hold it just as much as I had before.

Karen could tell, and she thrust the child at me. 'Her name's Rosie,' she said.

I'd only held a baby once before. Rosie felt soft and warm. She smelt of milk and strawberry jam. Her arms and legs were far stronger than I'd ever imagined they'd be. I didn't know how to hold her properly and she could tell. She pedalled her legs, banging her chubby knees against me, letting me know I wasn't doing it right. I stared into her eyes, and after sizing me up, she opened her mouth and smiled. There it was again, that tooth.

I started to cry.

When the others got back from the pub, Karen drove me up to the lay-by where Sarah and Mel had said they'd wait. As we got close by, I wondered what I'd do if they weren't there. But the peace sign on the bonnet of the ambulance shone, luminous, from miles away in the beam of Karen's headlights.

'Look after yourself,' she said, as I got out of the car. She smiled, but I could see her mind already starting to focus on all the things she'd have to do when she got back home. She did a u-turn and accelerated away. I stood there, listening to the sound of her car until I couldn't hear it anymore. Until I couldn't hear anything much at all.

Then I started to listen, to really listen. To the dandelion clocks along the edge of the road, swaying just a little bit in the breeze. To the hedge that shivered as a small animal passed. To the beat of my heart.

'Look after yourself,' I repeated under my breath.

Aisling Tempany

The Biography of Dorothy Edwards
as pencilled in a first edition of Rhapsody

Suicide @ 31

What else is there to know?

Perhaps why she stopped typing on that typewriter
Up in David Garnett's loft?

Or the name of the cellist
Who wouldn't leave his wife for her.

Some people are keen to know
What she burnt in the garden
On the day she died?

What great novel was lost that day?

I myself am only curious to know
How when she went to kill herself
She wasn't wearing any shoes?

Welsh writing in English

If you want to know about Welsh writing in English,
And you do, or you wouldn't be reading this,
You'll need to know the following:

There are lots of men called Williams and Thomas,
Studied by men called Williams and Thomas.
Some of them speak Welsh, and some of them don't
Some of them are born in Wales, and some of them aren't.
(Some of them are lying, some of them aren't.)

There are names like Gwyn and Glyn.
There's a Gwyn Jones and a Glyn Jones.
Glyn Jones is the good one!
There's also Gwyn Williams
But that's a bit too much to take.

You should expect to see names like:
Richards, Lewis or Davies.
You'll even see the name Richard Lewis Davies
Or Lewis Richard Davies
And Lewis Davies too. They're all one man.

Jones, Evans, Roberts.
These are the names of Welsh Writing.
You should probably come from Wales, actually.
If you're not, perhaps you should change your name
Try to sound more Welsh, like Peggy Whistler.

If you really want to know about
Welsh writing in English
This is what you should know.
And if you're not interested in that
Well, why exactly are you here?

Because the Revolution will not come

Because the Revolution will not come
I poured a kettle of water on my arm.
It didn't hurt, it didn't hurt at all
It just looks a little red.

Because the Revolution will not come
I cut my finger on a piece of glass
And held it in the rain to bruise.
It turned my finger purple.

Because the Revolution will not come
I sit and hurt myself instead
Making my skin go red or purple
The world goes on the same. So do I.

Marion McCready

The Captayannis

The Firth has birthed a sugar ship.
Cormorants as black as the Furies
have commandeered her starboard.

*A part of me crept inside her
while she slept in my womb,
smaller than a plum.
I imagined I could keep her buried
like a treasure. But even the Captayannis
could not keep her cargo.*

Beached on sand banks, she has leaked
Caribbean cane for thirty years.
She has turned the river to syrup.

*I've been awake for days,
the window translates morning
into my room. Clouds glide like continents
above the yacht-mottled Clyde.
I daydream of cormorants
and crystalline, plums with apple seed hearts.*

The Greenock girls in their silver heels
do not see the sugar ship.
She has been there all their lives.

Child

The field has drowned and turned
into a tideless sea.
> *Flower shapes rise from*
> *a toddler's broken ribs.*

Beyond the head of a loch
a broken swing hangs from a tree.
> *His body bruises in the dark,*
> *he has learned to be quiet.*

Clouds drag their shadows
over hills, ridges, fields of sheep.
> *His eyes are the colour of fists,*
> *he has learned to be still.*

I'm up to my knees in nothing
but the bare November breeze.
> *His hand prints on the windowpanes,*
> *the trail of his sticky sleeves.*

I'm chasing after the cat's eyes
of a child I cannot see.
> *Where have all the leaves gone,*
> *where are the streets of leaves?*

Life Rafts

The pier lights glow like gas lamps
in the darkening twilight sky.
Silver railings slice the Firth

into manageable bites.
My pockets are packed with leaves.
Not a breath of air to breathe.

Should you have to abandon ship

Street lights throw vertical columns
of orange into the shallows.
The hills behind the river town

are lit like a circuit board.
The drone of a ferry drawing in,
the soundtrack of going home.

Should you have to abandon ship

Stars are growing on the Firth.
They are pouring from my mouth.
I unfold my hand, a ticket falls

but does not reach the ground.
A pier-hand ushers us on
and somewhere deep inside me calls:

Should you have to abandon ship…

Lizzie Fincham

Heading For The Coast

A woman looks out at frost on a field.
He left yesterday.

Didn't take much. Travelling light.
Heading for the coast.

Collected Love-In-The-Mist Seeds

Collected love-in-the-mist seeds
today into three jam jars I found under the sink.

In Welsh the word ynys means an island
but in Cornish it also means an isolated place.

Outside the morning glory is still playing
Jack and the Beanstalk

reaching above the wall
looking for more light.

I've cut down the remnants
of the lemon hollyhock,

which I'd saved with a splint.
I fill and refill the zinc watering-can,

dead-head the nasturtiums
hearing the life-rattle

of their hard green pods
falling onto the stones

under my feet.

Two Sheets

Recently we've compared notes.
All three of us have obsessively

captured every last text message
you sent us in those small spaces

between procedures,
blood and temperature checks,

changes of fluid bags
and the increasing fogs

of intravenous morphine and pain.
Two of us have used books with marbled pages,

the other, just two sheets
of handmade paper.

Rule of Thumb
Amy Shuckburgh

I don't play bingo and I've never gambled, but I've got a strange relationship with numbers. It's not that I'm great at maths. I still count on my fingers to do my times-tables. I work out my nines by holding both hands in front of me and counting along, bending the finger down at the right point, figuring out the answer from the fingers left standing. But that's not the kind of number stuff I'm talking about. I mean numbers cropping up at significant moments, things happening that make you think, and once you start thinking, the stranger the coincidences seem.

Sevens kicked in when I started working in the chemist. Every sale ended with a seven, or had a seven somewhere, hand on hip, leaning jauntily, 'nonchalant', as Karly would say.

'Isn't that weird,' I whispered to one of the girls as we were cashing up. I wouldn't have mentioned anything, except the takings had come to £377.77. 'And all my receipts today ended in a seven.' She just smiled and carried on thumbing the notes.

I got the bus home and every number-plate had a seven in it, or numbers which added up to seven, or divided down to seven. When you walk, you can count things, measure them out: the lamp posts you pass, the times your foot crosses a crack. I counted the stairs to my room, cars passing in the street, how often the word GOD was used in our house.

When I was younger, I imagined myself standing in the middle of a circle, with spokes going out from the centre. On each of those spokes stood a person in my life. If everyone stood equally distanced from me at the centre then the circle would spin evenly. There were seven spokes on the wheel: my mum, my dad, my mum's boyfriend, my dad's girlfriend, my two brothers and my friend, Karly, who was my brother's girlfriend, on and off. Karly was sixteen then and told me what to do with boys when I got older, how to act grown-up, 'nonchalant' she called it.

Karly wore a leather jacket and had pink hair in little dreadlocks. Sometimes she baby-sat, staying in my brother's room, when he was away at boarding school. The doorbell would always ring.

'It's alright, Debs,' she'd say. 'It's for me.'

Different men turned up and followed Karly upstairs.

'You watch cartoons, Debs, I'll be down in a bit.'

I'd loiter on the landing until she came out and said: 'Why don't you be the secretary?' She showed me how to write the names of the men in my school jotter, the times they arrived and left. I felt important. I started grading them out of ten. I thought it would be great to be liked by so many men, to be able to chose, like Karly could.

I told that story years later to Hedge. 'Didn't you twig?' he said. 'She was working.' I looked blank. 'You were keeping records of her turnover,' he laughed.

Karly was large-boned, her chin and forehead were pimply, her eyes hooded. She wasn't pretty, but all along I'd thought they liked her leather jacket.

I had a crush on my maths teacher at school. He was called Mr Triole. He'd touch my shoulder in class, or make a remark on the height of my skirt. There was no uniform and I was beginning to try out different versions of myself. I put outfits together that clashed. I didn't want to be one of the others, just a number. I wasn't a maths-type of person, but Mr Triole used to stop me after class. He tapped the top of my file, which I held up in front of me, guarding my chest.

'Was I planning on doing Maths A-level?' And, 'Had I thought about extra lessons?' Then, 'Did I want a lift home?'

I blushed and mumbled something. When I got home, I told my mum. She said: 'He won't do anything'. And he didn't. Well not then, anyway.

By the time I got the job in the chemist, I was dead-set on renting a flat on my own. I was saving for a deposit and for luck I decided to keep my bank-balance always ending in a seven.

Hedge's real name was Leslie. He liked touching and all the usual things, but he also liked sitting and watching the river, or lying on his bed listening to music. We discussed things we wanted to do, like drive a camper-van to the edge of a cliff.

It was all going nicely, until I got the flat.

The address was 22 Swan Lane. Well, like I said, I've never played, but I do know that two swans a-swimming is the name they give to twenty-two in Bingo. It felt lucky. I handed over my hard-earned money. I was only 21, but I was waiting for the numbers to align. I knew when they did, things would start happening.

Near the flat was an underpass that crossed four lanes of traffic, whizzing westwards. Someone had scrawled on the concrete walls: 'Two million dead' in pink paint. I began to see other words in the lettering.

'A million beads.'

'Two miles of diamonds.'

You can make your own sense out of things when you try hard enough.

I quit the job at the chemist and got offered a position at an erotic magazine, filing mainly, and answering calls. 'You're going to let dirty old men slobber over you,' Hedge said.

I rolled my eyes.

'Did you know that elephants die thirty years early when they live in captivity?'

Hedge shrugged and said:

'Did you know that if you eat alone, you die alone.'

Since I'd moved into the flat, Hedge had started to complain. About the flat. About me. Said the place smelt of damp. Said it reminded him of an old people's home. It was true, there were dried stains on the brown carpet and it smelt of mould. We decided to split up. But then he started showing up late at night. I would hear him call my name through the blur of sleep.

'Debs!'

It was Friday, 22 February. That's already three twos.

'Debs!'

I thought I heard the word 'Beads', and imagined the pink lettering scuttering off the walls. The underpass tilted and the beads slid up and down like an abacus, counting out the calls, then counting out the space between the calls. I opened my eyes and looked at my watch. It was twelve minutes past twelve; you couldn't make this up.

I went outside to speak to him, but the street was empty. I went and stood in the underpass in my dressing gown and read: 'Divide your mission'. I suppose I was looking for an answer.

The thesaurus at school started with a section called Abstract Reasoning. It began with Existence, followed by 'Non-Existence. The section on Numbers came between Order and

Time. Someone made those decisions. Hedge said 'Could we be friends and meet sometimes for lunch'. I said 'Fine', but I couldn't help looking for meaning everywhere. Whenever I looked at my watch it would always be two minutes, or twenty two minutes or thirty-two minutes past the hour.

For instance, it was exactly 2.22pm when Hedge said:

'Don't you love the feeling when you've had something lodged in your teeth since lunch and you finally work it loose with your tongue?'

I looked at him.

'It doesn't taste of anything, but it's a relief. You know?'

The job at the erotic magazine was paying my rent. Sometimes gentlemen would call, wanting titillating conversation. I sat in my subscriptions corner, flicking through back-issues. The articles were erotic all right. I read a story about a girl on a train who sat opposite a man carrying a silver walking cane. Eventually she let him part her legs with the cane, while the train jiggled across the countryside. Well, you can guess the rest. By lunchtime, I felt odd throbbings inside my jeans.

I met Hedge for a sandwich and I was just about to tell him about the silver cane, when across the street, I saw Mr Triole.

'Oh my god.'

Mr Triole, who I hadn't seen since my GCSEs. Mr Triole, who'd once pinged my bra strap.

'What?' Hedge asked.

'Nothing,' I took another bite of my sandwich. Hedge went back to his job at the coffee shop, where he made flat whites and piccolos. I pretended to send a text, but Mr Triole had seen me and was crossing the street.

'Hello, Debs.'

I looked up, nonchalant as you like.

'Hello, Mr Triole.'

We went for a coffee at Hedge's competition. Mr Triole asked if I'd been keeping up with my maths. He said, why didn't I consider doing Maths A-level, never too late?

'No thanks,' I said.

That night I had a dream that Mr Triole was giving a maths lesson in the underpass. He was using the wall as a blackboard, working out sums in pink paint. We were counting to a million and by the time I woke, we'd got to seven thousand, seven hundred and seventy seven. The shock of all those sevens again must have jolted me awake.

The gentleman subscriber rang the office again the next day. I hung up, wondering if I'd been rude, or encouraging. Then the phone rang again. It was a voice I recognised, but a different voice. It was Mr Triole.

'I'd like to have supper with you,' he said. 'It's not weird because you're not my student now.'

'How'd you get my number?'

'Will you have supper with me?' Mr Triole asked again.

'I'm not interested in maths. I'm interested in Astrology,' I said, to set him straight. 'And poetry.'

'That's all right'.

At his house he talked about words. 'You'd be surprised how interesting mathematical terms can be,' Mr Triole said. 'Numbers can be variable or complex, they can be irrational or transcendental.'

He poured more wine. His flat was peculiarly neat. We sat side by side on the beige sofa.

'Mathematicians talk about all sorts of interesting things that are a bit like poetry. Like matrices, harmonics, algorithms...' I watched his mouth round the words. They sounded like exotic dances.

'What number would I be?' I was flushed from the wine.

'You'd be an ordinal number.' He said, looking at me over the top of his glasses.

'I'd rather be a prime number.' My words were slurring. 'And you can be an odd number.'

'All right.' He smirked and leant forward. We were suddenly kissing.

'Did you do a PhD?' I asked, pulling back.

'No,' he looked glum, pushing the glasses up his nose. 'I got stuck on the concepts of real and natural numbers.' He trailed off.

'Is there a difference?'

'Oh God, yes,' he said. 'They're worlds away.'

We went back to kissing. He tasted of yoghurt and his face scratched. His hand moved up my leg, like a doctor feeling for tissue damage.

I didn't want to be there. The place smelt of hairspray, a whiff of socks beneath.

'Don't go,' he said.

Out on the street I couldn't think where I was. I looked for buses. The 98, the 41, the 109. The numbers didn't mean anything to me. I thought of Hedge. Tears sprang into my eyes and I tried laughing, to splutter them away.

Suddenly I saw Karly walking towards me. The wide face and hooded eyes, though she wore a baseball cap, so I couldn't see her pink hair.

'Karly,' I called. 'It's me.' She looked blank. 'Debs,' I prompted.

It wasn't Karly. She sneered and pushed past. I started crying again. The crying and the walking eventually led me back to the Bayswater Road. I knew my way home from there.

'Money is really about trust. Trust and fear, and fear only exists in our imagination. So basically money is imaginary.' I looked at him. I wasn't sure I followed the argument, but I nodded and took another sip of my shandy. 'Nothing isn't such an easy concept to get your head around,' he went on. 'For instance, what happens when you add zero to the number five?'

I blinked. 'You still have five,' I said, feeling relieved.

'Ok. But what happens when you multiply zero and five?'

I swallowed, concentrating on the ceiling.

'You get zero,' Hedge blurted out, triumphant.

I rolled my eyes and yawned. I thought maybe I did like Mr Triole, after all.

The erotic magazine was all paper-work and avoiding discussions about erect nipples. I read my stars obsessively so I wouldn't be to blame for my decisions. I stopped wearing a watch so I couldn't check the time every thirty seconds. I kept coming back to the idea that the certainty of mathematics was the answer. I called Mr Triole to tell him and we met in The Ship and drank shandies overlooking the swill of river-water caught between the barges. I looked into his eyes bulging behind the thick panes of his glasses.

'Loyalty in the workplace is cheaper than performance incentives,' the editor was saying. The magazine was folding. People were still reading erotic stories. But it was the margins, they just didn't add up. I sat in on the meeting, doodling Gerald

Triole's name on my jotter. Sometimes, to ring the changes, I'd doodle *Hedge* instead. Then I tried *Leslie*, but I saw the words *lie* and *sell*, and scribbled it out. I wrote *Mr and Mrs Triole* a few times, but that made me feel weird.

'I'm terribly sorry,' the editor went on. 'But I'm forced...by circumstances ...out of my control.'

We had all lost our jobs. Hedge picked me up and carried a box of my belongings. On top was my jotter. *Gerald Triole* was written on the cover, surrounded by hearts. Next to it, about twenty-two times, I'd written *Debs Triole* in different styles.

'What the hell? ' Hedge looked at me. I stared straight ahead. I'd counted to nineteen in my head before he said again, 'What the hell!'

I felt the spinning wheel of my life with me in the middle and the seven spokes lolloping by, skewed and off-kilter.

The day I turned twenty-two began oddly. I was woken by muffled calls and for a moment I couldn't remember who was lying next to me, Hedge or Mr Triole. I studied the pale pimply skin, black hairs sprouting from the shoulder-blades. I reached my mind back to remember.

The night before spun in my head. Hedge had dropped the box onto the pavement and shouted words like *vulgar* and *square root* at me. A bus passed. It was the 207, my bus home, the bus containing both my numbers, separated by the great hollow of zero, nothing, the absence of things.

I stood in a silent circle of space on the pavement, the action flurrying around me. Hedge opened the jotter. Inside he read: *Reasons to like Hedge* alongside *Reasons to like Mr Triole*. It was the mathematical order of my thinking that hurt the most, he said. Who had I become? What about the camper-van on the cliffs, listening to the waves?

I grabbed the jotter and turned to a page where I'd written a giant *H* and an enormous *T*.

The H, I'd decided, was a good solid letter, balanced, like a bridge.

The T also looked all right: protective, steady, rooted.

'But look,' I hiccupped. 'See, I circled the word *bridge* and put hearts round the H,' I showed him. 'I chose *you*. It's not only numbers, it's letters too. Like the Chinese drawing for the word for house.'

He looked at me like I was mad.

'You're mad,' he spat and walked away, slipping in and out of the wet triangles of street-lamps.

I picked up my box and waited for my bus. I got off at my stop and walked through my underpass. 'To win he's fled,' I read in the pink graffiti on the wall.

I found Mr Triole on my doorstep. 'Happy Birthday, Debs,' he grinned. He held a ceramic swan under one arm. He pressed his beard and lips against my mouth.

So it was Mr Triole in my bed. I wriggled under the covers. My name came again through the damp wall. Gerald groaned and rolled over.

Outside I found Hedge. His eyes were red from crying.

'Why did you do it?' he squeaked.

'I don't know,' I said. 'I was hoping it would become clear.'

We went and sat in the underpass together, listening to cars swishing westward, heading towards the sea. I didn't even bother counting them.

Lyn White

Games

The National Socialists have played with us for a long time in the Westerbork mouse-trap.
                    Diary of Philip Mechanicus Tuesday February 1st 1944

You have to be lucky here—for as long as it lasts.
Diary of Philip Mechanicus Sunday February 6th 1944

The rules are easy.
The game may change.
You may not use pavements
or certain shops,
these are for Aryans only
as are trams, bicycles and all woodland.

The aim is to avoid being left
with the yellow star.
This is an unlucky suit.
Dodge spades and clubs,
they mean different things here.
Diamonds are useful
can buy you time.
Hearts are out of place.

In the grand tournament
opportunity to seize a piece
is never missed. There are
no genuine flight squares
for refuge, but
on the way round
you may land on a chance
to apply for exemption
deferment, even Aryanization.

If you choose this last option
you pass immediately
to the medical section
for measurement of your cranium
assessment of nose shape, eye colour
to trace suspect antecedents
and your place in the chain.

There is no adjournment.
Eventually all yellow stars
board the train and go east.
The endgame is over
when they have been taken.

Westerbork Transit Camp

As flies carry infectious diseases, every camp resident is under obligation to catch fifty per day and deliver them, wrapped in a piece of paper, to the Quarantine Station.
　　　　　　　　　Diary of Philip Mechanicus, Sunday July 25th 1943

Did you swish the warm air
open your hand to corpses
squashed, black, lying in your palm
and count how close you'd come?
Maybe there were competitions
among the others,
even a sardonic laugh to relieve the tension.
Perhaps you marked up five-bar gates
plotted a comic chart or graph.
Sometimes it might have helped
wile away the days of fear
waiting for your name
to appear on one of the endless lists
that would transport you
from Holland into Poland
from where no news, no letters ever came.
More likely, I believe, you watched them
swarm across your table, fist frozen, gaze fixed
on despised creatures innocently engaged
swatted by anyone and everyone.

Gull

I can stand and look at the gulls for long periods on end—they are the symbol of true freedom. They take off from the ground whenever they want to ...
Diary of Philip Mechanicus, Thursday July 29th 1943

Being a birder I note, from your entry,
the time of year and the deft word-sketch
which gives the jizz.
They were Black-headeds
so, this morning,
I don't have to stretch my mind
to find you, you come to life
across the lake in another gull
that's roosted through another time
waited until now to tell me,
when I need to hear it most,
you are not lost,
you discovered flight
before they pushed you on the train.
You left the ground, soared, hovered
one eye tilted over the loaded cattle trucks
surprised to find you weren't on board
and for a while glided as it shunted east
then peeled off before its final stop.
You've been recovered in this red-billed,
red-legged individual to delight my heart,
set it at rest in the dark, chocolate hood
and pale plumage of a seagull's breast.

Klompen
Klompen is the Dutch word for clogs

In the past few days, owing to incessant rain, the camp has become a great pool of mud through which one must literally wade. Anyone who has clogs goes about in clogs ...
                    Diary of Philip Mechanicus, Friday November 12th 1943

Mud, nothing but mud.
                    Diary of Philip Mechanicus, Wednesday November 24th 1943

Yesterday evening I had another chance of escaping on a train to Amsterdam. Dead easy. But I was wearing clogs...
                    Diary of Philip Mechanicus, Thursday February 3rd 1944

Tonight you churn my sleep
as you turn over the mud
of an endless swamp
that stretches through the camp.
You go from hut to hut,
gait awkward with effort,
learning to keep clogs firm on feet
that sink in channels of sludge.
I hear the suck, see you pluck
your willow shoes from bogs
that glisten slime in relentless rain
feel the strain of toes clamped
to clutch heels on wood
as you struggle out.
You plough through the quag,
stout, Dutch klompen inching lower.
You drag ankle, knee,
flag thigh-deep in a mire so dense
even your tenacity is useless.
Your arms squirm to keep your head
above the quaking silt
hope closes over you, you are gone.
I wake empty handed,
the clag of history leaving me
no rope to throw you.

Frances-Anne King

Trace

You could argue it was nothing,
only the murk of shadows; traffic's echo

through the city's narrow alleys, old stories
sifting images across my mind.

Maybe the past did come back to meet me —
someone I'd loved, some ancestor calling

blood to blood. How can you know
that time didn't slip like a child from a swing,

leaving that sound of chains in the wind,
and an empty seat full of presence.

Lost Constellation
For Emma

Light plays her skin;
gentles the taut line of cheek bone,
dusts her dropped lids
cradles the angle of her jaw

and weaves her pale hair
in the shadows she prefers,
as head bent, her fingers
slot a puzzle into place.

Light floods her eyes
as standing close she searches yours
for her lost constellation—
turning in a distant galaxy—

and when the seizure strikes
and her eyes blank,
her hands hold yours,
as if to gift you her endurance.

Roman Uncle

On the cusp of evening
we walked together
down a street where shadows clustered,
to the wine store.
You swept aside the curtain
and we stepped into the claustral cool,
where I scuffed my shoes through sawdust
to make patterns in the shavings
so the night beasts wouldn't catch me.

I ran my fingers round the rims of barrels,
watched as pale wine was poured
into carafes—the pungency of wood
and wine enclosed me.
Outside you swung me to your shoulders,
sang *Santa Lucia* through the cigarette
and coffee scented dusk.
You stopped to cough—
death meant nothing to me then.

Bart's at Five a.m.

Winter is the hardest. That feeling
of slow deconstruction when the edge of you

gives a little, starts to crumble,
as light seeps through ward windows,

blots up the dark, touching beds,
lockers, sleeping patients, with a grained

film of grey and white. Air flickers—
blurred and jagged at the edges

like a silent movie, and here, in this
no-man's-land, time suddenly seems

negotiable. Then the rumble of meat lorries
across the square in Smithfield

hooks you back to the now,
to the cold leaking through you,

to the sound of bodies breathing
through the slow haemorrhage of dawn.

Jane McLaughlin

August on the River

The river breeds its own gods, russet-skinned,
blue-skulled, blue-tattooed, circles of sun
in gold around their necks. Big diesels twinned
in the shimmering wake beat a great drum.
Above, the red-rinsed mothers reclining
like goddesses on decks of snow-washed craft.
A pack of Fosters, system loud, the shining
of flying water, diamonds scattered aft.
The nymphs are golden, ponytailed and fair.
White jeans, big earrings, big designer shades.
Their laughter carries on the cooling air
and mobiles chorus as the daylight fades.
Along the banks red charcoal fires glow;
meteors fly, the stars walk bright and slow.

St Anthony at Baiardo

There are designer saints, but he's not one of them,
  his quake-cracked hilltop shrine open to the sky,
lace of the bridal bouquets
  grown tatty in the wind and sun.

Above the ravine padded with rich shrubs
that vanish in darkness below trees,
  sounds of calm lives and work drift up to him
like slow bubbles: chopping wood, whistling,
a dog's cheerful bark.
  He guards the stillness
of land that leaps and splits,
  tips streets into rubble, hurls rocks.

He keeps good company:
  a Chinese sailor who came with the Saracens
looks down from a pillar;
  under a stone slab lies a Sanremese artist who
"brought young and old to a better
  and more beautiful world"

Beyond the church the grass
  dances with lapis and opal:
cicadas that flash blue as they leap
  vault and flicker in the green —
peacock dragonflies jet off
  over the precipice
towards the moon-white faces
  of the Alpi Liguri.

Every few seasons the ancient
  terraced land burns to black stumps.
Small new olive trees
  show green along the roads.
He minds the quietness
  between fire and fire, earthquake and quake.

Beside a pile of hacked cypress branches
  two men sit on the stepped path to the church
  with a carafe of dark wine
finishing the afternoon.

Twilight's Baby
Sue Vickerman

It's full moon, and Twilight is in labour.

Meanwhile I'm crouched behind a bush, doing the watch. I finish rolling a fag, quick as lightening in my fingerless gloves, second nature, then flick open my lighter. The flare sets off jumping shadows in the undergrowth beyond the floodlit strip that marks out the fence's perimeter.

Suddenly I'm running.

Approaching the encampment I see a new vehicle, a VW camper, pulled in by my truck. Three shapes are hunched in scattered picnic chairs around the campfire. Must be three more over-nighters. The fourth person, all legs, jumping about like Pippi Longstocking on speed, is Lucy.

'Luce.'

She comes out of the circle to meet me. Lucy dropped out of university for this. Her mother sometimes joins us, bringing a mountain of non-perishable food in Tupperware.

'I don't know what's wrong with me. I suddenly got the creeps over there.'

Lucy's eyes go big.

'I personally would be perfectly happy to leave a child alone with my Rottweiler,' a Welsh accent is saying. 'It's men who turn them to violence. They're a very loving breed, in a feminist's hands.'

The woman notices me and Luce looking at her, and beams.

'I'm a professional dog-handler, see.'

I'm not prejudiced but they bring it on themselves, sometimes, the Welsh.

Lucy is putting a mug of PG Tips into my hand, winking. I can see the others are dandling camomile or peppermint or something on bits of string in their cups.

'These women have come for the solstice, Scottie,' explains Lucy.

I hear apology in her voice. The things that bring women here. It's a madhouse, sometimes. I ask where they're from.

'Anglesey,' says the one with all the hair. 'We're the Anglesey Witches' Coven. I'm Gaia, by the way, and that there is Gwynneth, and this is Sand.'

I scrutinise the blissed-out, dreadlocked woman next to plump, pink Gwynneth. Purple DMs. Loads of ragged skirts. And she's rolling up, a beatific smile on her face. There's got to be weed in there.

'That Sand as in Sandra?' I ask, doubting it.

'No, actually. Sand as in Sand. Waves crashing on the sand, as in. And you are?'

She's smiling at me from under her dreads, shivering a bit. Thin as a rail under all those rainbow layers. They fancy me, her type. 'Scottie,' I tell her.

Lucy lassoes me with a possessive arm. 'She's from Inverurie.'

'Lucy's told us there's a baby on the way in that shelter,' burbles Gwynneth.

In the distance, a dome made of bent willow branches covered over in plastic is glowing with candlelight. Milky shapes are moving within: Twilight's helpers; the midwife types.

'It's fantastic,' breathes Gaia, 'it's like, *wow* - we've been led here to share in this.'

It seems that Gaia is their Mother Superior, or whatever.

'I feel there's magic in the air,' says Gwynneth.

So she feels something, too. Not that I believe in magic.

'They might be expecting a delivery,' suggests Lucy, scanning the sky above the airfield.

'What a coincidence,' quips Gwynneth.

'Nothing is a coincidence,' says Gaia, in a manner that we're supposed to find both wise and mysterious. 'It *is* the solstice.'

She's English, not Welsh. The worst kind. From Down South.

'How's Twilight doing?' I ask Lucy, nodding at the distant shelter.

'Oh, god,' Lucy flusters. 'She's doing well, apparently; only, I don't know much about it, technically speaking. They're rubbing her back and things.'

Gaia gives Lucy a smile that says - you have no idea.

'I keep taking in tea,' Lucy apologises.

The newcomers, like all the short-termers, are reaching out

their hands to the fire. They've taken up that huddled position, chins inside jackets.

'One thing that *is* different,' bounces Lucy, 'is that their patrol car has come over to the fence and peered at us no less than three times in the last hour.'

'It's possible they've picked up about Twilight starting labour,' I theorise.

'You mean, they've got spies, or what?' asks Gwynneth.

'We don't know exactly. It's just, sometimes they seem to know stuff. Like, when an action is planned, they're waiting for us. Whatever point we go in around all those miles of fencing, they seem to have been tipped off.'

The witches stare hard into the thicket.

'It could be some kind of radio reception. Picking up our voices from a long distance with ultra-sensitive equipment,' I say vaguely. 'We don't really know.' I'm feeling uneasy again. When you confront the fact that they can blow up the planet, you start to think they can do anything.

'So, but what do you do, if you realise they're up to something, like? Out on the base, I mean?' asks Gwynneth excitedly. 'I mean, what do we all do?'

'Bastards,' throws in the huddled shape of Sand. Her tongue flicks, licking a Rizla.

'Normally we keep a watch so we can send out phone messages about new planes landing,' Lucy explains. 'Like, the type of plane; whether it's a missile carrier, or whatever. And obviously we watch the gates for if anything's sent out. Especially during the night. The biggest convoys have always left during the night.'

'Is that when you do blockades?' asks Gwynneth. She's got a fairly practical turn of mind for a witch.

'Now the weather's gone cold we haven't got enough women to do blockading. Apart from at weekends,' I explain. 'That's probably why the last convoy took off midweek. All we could do was phone round; track it across the country. Get the network to watch out. There was only me and Luce and Cayote here at the time. The others had gone to town for a bath.'

Gaia, who wandered off to stick her head in Twilight's shelter a few minutes ago, reappears from the shadows and stands in a position where the fire up-lights her face. Her eye sockets are dark pools.

'The wolf is here,' she announces. 'I've just seen the baby's totem. He's here, giving protection.' Gaia flops back into a plastic picnic chair.

I wonder what she does for her day-job.

'I reckon Twilight's got a couple of hours to go yet,' she's saying, 'which would make it - let's see - a midnight baby. Bang on the solstice. Fantastic. Something really special is going on here tonight, women. I can feel it.'

'It's what *they're* up to that worries me.' I jerk a thumb over my shoulder at the fence. 'We've only got my truck, your camper and Twilight's Morris Minor if they decide to bring something out. End to end we would probably reach across the exit road at the main gate, but without back-up, they'll tow us off in a matter of minutes. It'd be a bit pointless.'

'Nothing's pointless!' cries Lucy in her Famous Five way, cheeks flushed from doing stretching. 'It's a protest, isn't it? It's still non-violent direct action. It holds them up, but more important, it makes a statement. We will not sit idly by and watch this madness. We are reclaiming our tomorrow!'

I can't say that stuff without feeling a right plonker. I just feel it. 'Yeh,' I say, quietly. 'Yeh.'

'Well I think we should start by doing a white-light ritual,' says Gaia. 'That child needs to be born into a safe space. We need to create that safe space; get some protection around this encampment.'

'First things first: I'm up for another cuppa. Anyone else?' If they're doing one of these circling, chanting affairs, I'm going to busy myself with the fire.

'I think we should decide what to do about the base first. Set out our plan for the whole night,' says Lucy firmly, 'in case they *do* know about the baby, and think we're all distracted.'

'Should we be planning to blockade, in case anything does come out?' asks Gwynneth with urgency. 'I mean, decide who'll drive the three vehicles,' - as if anyone else is going to get their hands on my truck - 'and decide who'll stay back here?'

I don't want to dampen Gwynneth's enthusiasm, but we need to warn her.

'You do know it's dangerous,' Lucy starts.

'That last demo,' I say. 'When we had the twenty thousand

here. Women got injured, you know.'

Gwynneth is looking excessively horrified already.

'As the missile launcher was creeping forward out of the main gate, a bunch of us ran out and lay in front of it. It was a kind of tank, the size of two double-decker buses. It wasn't going to stop. Me and Lucy got away in the nick of time. They'd have gone over us. We had to take one woman to hospital with a broken ankle.'

Gwynneth shudders. 'What - a wheel went over her?'

'Actually no. As she was running away, she fell in the campfire pit. Bloody lucky there wasn't a fire at the time.'

Gaia has been sitting all this time in a meditational pose with her eyes closed. Now she opens them, doing this calm, guru-type thing, until she's got us all looking at her.

'We've brought something with us which will stop them coming out of the gate at all,' she says.

'Oh God - ' Gwynneth chirps. 'The menstrual blood. Of course. I mean God*dess*.'

'Jeezus Christ.' It just slips out. Grabbing the kettle in my glove I retreat to the shadows to get a refill of water from the canister.

Beyond the thicket, beyond the fence, far off, I sense a kind of hum; an energy. Something like a vibrating generator. I shiver, slopping the water about.

This is stupid. It's *Gaia* who's spooking me. Self-styled posh witch. I bet she comes from Surrey.

Stepping back into the flickering warmth of the campfire I find myself alone. I put the kettle on the makeshift hotplate, squat, and get my baccy out, listening to the soft drone of Gaia's voice chanting incantations in the ring of darkness beyond the firelight. I watch the stumbling shapes of Gaia, Gwynneth, Sand and Lucy make a slow circle around the camp.

I'm the one who gets all these women's decrepit cars going after they've conked out sitting in the damp overnight. I'm the wood-gatherer; the all-night watch. I don't go for the daft rituals; the singing. Not that I've got anything against it. It's people making themselves feel secure.

I take a drag on my roll-up, feeling chill prickles down my spine.

When everyone's back in the cosy picnic circle, I feel okay again. Witchcraft is typical English shite, anyway. These women have been duped.

The latest report on Twilight is being offered. Something about the dilation of her cervix; I don't need the details.

'So. This menstrual blood. Is it in a bucket?' I ask conversationally, passing round a packet of Hobnobs.

'Twit,' laughs Gwynneth, 'It's used tampons. We've been saving them up, haven't we girls?'

Gaia's smile towards Gwynneth has a kind of glitter behind it.

'I mean, *women*,' Gwynneth corrects herself.

Gross. Unbelievably *gross*. I try to maintain an inscrutable expression.

'What I suggest is this,' intones Gaia. 'We take our blood, and place it on the main gates. It *is* the solstice. There's nothing more potent against male negative energy than women's creative blood. Believe me, they'll be terrified by it. They'll never break through that barrier on this night. A blockade will not be necessary.'

'Cool,' murmurs Sand blissfully.

'And that's the handy thing about tampons, see,' Gwynneth chimes in enthusiastically, 'its easy to pop them on the gates - just tie them on with the string!'

Lucy looks a bit crestfallen. 'I don't like to give up the idea of blockading. It's more visible; more of a stand. Even though we've only three piddling vehicles at the moment. They'd still have the hassle of moving us.'

Gaia reaches over to Lucy and caresses her cheek. 'Have faith, Lucy. They won't be able to come out through the main gate tonight.'

Lucy volunteers to stay at the campfire in case of visitors, so it's down to me to lead the witches through the thicket to the main gate.

The first ten minutes of walking brings us to the monitoring spot near what used to be a back entrance. The old gates are netted over with ivy and creeping weeds. The women's horrified whispers, on seeing the fence, remind me of how menacing it looked to me that first time, its coils of razor-wire stretching for miles and miles.

Then I see it. A sort of glow; a kind of floodlit effect. 'Look,' I whisper, the night air creeping down the back of my neck. 'Over by the airfield. That weird light.'

'What's this hanging on this twig?' whispers Gwynneth. 'I've got some wrapped round my arm.'

'That's left from the last big demo,' I hiss. 'Whole thicket becomes one huge toilet.'

'Ugh, loo paper!' She starts thrashing about to release herself. 'Disgusting!'

Ordinarily I'd laugh, considering what she's carrying in her shoulder bag.

'Shshh.' Gaia stops Gwynneth. 'What's that?'

The undergrowth shuffles and crackles in the darkness. A breath of wind sifts leaves, detaching a few more from the branches where they've lived and died. A call resounds in the silence like an echo beneath a distant bridge.

'Sounds like a tannoy,' whispers Gwynneth.

I'm not the melodramatic type. Far from it. But what if they're flying them in? What if it's tonight? The peace camp isn't what it used to be. We no longer have the numbers. I look at the witches and sigh.

'Wish I'd brought my dog Barry,' says Gwynneth in a low voice behind me.

I'm appalled. 'We can't set Rottweilers onto them.'

'He's a Jack Russell!'

Gaia and I go 'Shshh.' Sand is unpicking her skirts from a bramble.

'Dogs can tell you things,' mutters Gwynneth, darkly.

After we pass the look-out point, the track is not so well-used. We move on slowly between clawing bushes, the sky ahead brightening with an orange glow. I sense Gaia at my elbow.

Arriving at the main gate we hang back beyond the band of light and I point out the cameras trained on the huge electronic gates. A broad road of pale gravel leads to the nearby A-road and, a few miles further on, the motorway. Inside the fence, across a hundred metres of land cemented flat and dotted with the hulks of army vehicles, is a concrete rotunda, the control tower. Tiny black figures are moving about in the brightly-lit glass box at the top. Beyond the control tower is a shadowy office-block camouflaged by a roof of turf, the nerve-centre of the base. And somewhere else, there are living quarters: whole families sleeping, eating, existing.

'We'll be well away before they can get a vehicle to us,' I whisper.

I imagine the guys watching their closed-circuit monitors. American accents, incredulous. 'What the...?' Zooming in on the women at the fence. 'Am I seeing this right?' Close-ups on the hands: fingers tying quick knots, moving along a few steps, taking another item from a pocket. 'You're not gonna believe this...'

It all happens pretty fast. The witches run out, adrenalin-fuelled, singing. In the space of a minute they've prettily decorated the gate, dancing, laughing. No sooner are they out in the glare of the lights than the movement among the ants in the tower intensifies. The witches are quickly finished, running back to me, elated, as a solitary figure emerges and saunters over to a parked landrover. Its headlights go on, its nose turns onto the tarmac, and it slides at a moderate pace towards the main gate.

I feel a bit let down. 'They're obviously not prioritising this,' I say to the breathless women.

Gaia is in the bushes, watching. 'He's getting out - look - he's having a closer look,' she hisses, delighted.

The soldier is on his mobile. 'Prick,' contributes Sand.

Abruptly, the soldier thrusts his phone back into his jacket, leaps into his landrover and heads for the tower at speed. As the faint, uneven echo of a tannoy message filters across the night air, a dozen dark figures hurry from the tower into vehicles. Further into the black hole of the base, flashing lights appear, moving swiftly across the land.

Gaia is cackling like a witch. 'Looks like our power's working already!'

'This could be it; something coming in by air,' I say. Apprehension wells inside me. I think of cosy autumn evenings in Inverurie in front of my mother's fire with my feet up, Nutella straight from the jar. I don't know how I came to be so far away from home. For the first time, it all feels futile.

I shake myself. 'We need to hurry,' I call. 'If we want to blockade, we should get back to the vehicles.'

Jogging back along the perimeter fence under cover of the thicket the witches are loud, reckless. It's the rush you get from doing actions. The fence twangs on the edge of my vision. The presence of the base is a throbbing in my head, tinnitus in my ears. It feels alive.

'Something *is* in the air,' I breathe. Gwynneth sees something in my face. She puts her arm round my shoulders.

'It's the baby. I felt her coming a few minutes ago,' beams Gaia, scrutinising her watch in the dark. 'Two minutes to midnight.'

Suddenly a flailing, long-limbed creature is crashing through the undergrowth. 'Scottie!'

Lucy's hair is sticking to her tears. I hold open my arms and she falls into them, like Ann relying on Dick in The Famous Five. 'Lucy! Luce.'

'Something awful,' sobs Lucy.

The clouds have hurtled away, leaving the moon glowering in a void. Lucy's choked up; can hardly speak.

Gwynneth turns moon-white. 'The baby…' she wimpers.

'Oh, the baby seems alright,' Lucy finally manages.

Sirens.

'*That's* what I mean,' wails Lucy, 'Come and see. Come *on.*'

We run, sprinting on the bright strip of mown turf by the fence because keeping ourselves hidden no longer seems relevant. Realising that Sand has feeble, anorexic legs under all those skirts, I reach out to pull her along. As I grab her arm, a strobing beam whips us from behind. Our shadows go helter-skelter as the beam sweeps sideways, stabbing at points in the thicket like an extra-terrestrial finger. The helicopter pulls at our hair, swooping and screaming like prehistoric birdlife, then lifts away, spiralling off. Ahead, the back gate, deserted for all the years I've been here, is bathed in floodlights. Trucks are pulling up in lines behind the razor-wire, and black figures with rifles dart between them. Loud-speakers blare. Among the scramble of robotic messages, an over-riding voice shrills Alert! Alert!

Sand screams, her face as white as bone. I lip-read her words, 'Something's coming!' as the roar of the helicopter plays a riff on the membranes inside my ears.

She's right. A dark rumble, almost an earth tremor, signals the approach of a land-bound creature.

Louder.

The disused back gate screeches like pain, its rusty components disengaging under the volition of some electronic mechanism. It slowly pulls open, ripping out bushes and turf sewn peacefully into it over the seasons. The strobe of the helicopter sweeps up the mossy track inside the base and spotlights the oncoming beast.

I grab for hands, squeezing tight. 'I think it's a launcher.'

The beast is moving, slow as a caterpillar, while camouflaged vehicles zip around it like flies.

Gaia does a maniacal laugh. 'We stopped them! We stopped them using the main gate, ha ha ha!' Her eyes glitter black.

I drop Gaia's hand, freaked, and clasp my head in my hands against the ear-splitting noise. Perhaps this is the beginning of the end. Lucy's expression has gone apocalyptically tragic. I need to tell her I love her.

Gwynneth shakes us both by our arms, frantic, trying to make us understand over the noise. 'I *think* I can hear a baby crying.'

We're half a mile from Twilight's shelter. Gwynneth must be mad.

Lucy frees herself from Gwynneth's grip, pointing. 'Look! Look!'

But Gwynneth has already dashed off in the direction of the encampment. A grotesque heap of metal, longer than a train carriage, is crossing the threshold onto our land on slow, dark wheels.

'Jeezus.' Lucy is transfixed.

The searchlight spins, blinding me. 'Gaia! Where's Gaia? Don't let her do anything crazy.' And then I somehow catch Gaia's voice, indistinct, trampled beneath the thunder of the airborne and landborne monsters. There she is, standing in long grass, mane of hair silhouetted, her arms raised to the moon, talking. She finishes off with a big yowl, like a wolf.

The next thing is, I hear tinkly singing in my ears. It's happened. I've finally lost it.

But no - it's Lucy. *Singing.* Her pretty voice is barely audible; tiny beneath the rumble and roar of war machines.

'We are not afrai, ai-aid...'

She's doing Joan Baez, she's doing Woodstock at a time like this.

Then, like a mad prophet, she bellows out, 'Women are *co-ming!*' She looks like Joan of Arc in the film. 'We're here for our children,' she cries out to the soldiers.

I pull her into a bear-hug until she's engulfed in my big jersey and my lips are in her hair.

'There's no point,' I shout into her ear. 'Come to Inverurie. Let's grow vegetables.'

I don't think she hears a word of it. She escapes from me, crying out at the men, the machinery: 'For our *children's* children!'

I tug at Lucy's arm. 'If they're going to blow up the planet, we may as well be home!'

But she doesn't even try to read my lips. 'We're all coming,' she's shouting. 'From everywhere!'

I notice Sand pinned against a small tree like a rag doll. Meanwhile Gaia has sprinted off towards Twilight's bender, punching digits on her witch's mobile. Calling for an ambulance, I hope.

The launcher is out, like a freed lion, prowling majestically towards the A-road, and Lucy is haring across the patch of no-man's land towards it.

I address her retreating back. A whisper. 'But what can women *do?*'

Linda Benninghoff

To My Mother

Last year
at this time
you fractured your back
again
and I brought you tea,
helped fix dinner,
went shopping,
put you to bed.

You have abandoned
so many gardens
and they grow wild.
A lone crocus
blooms in the front yard—
the rest of it hungry weed

I wonder how many
springs we will still
see together,
The roses in
the back undaunted
and gulping
light, this summer
as last summer,
the bruised wisteria
still clutching the base of the home.

My Hands

hold nothing. water
pouring to the dark earth
pushed by the wheels of cars and bicycles
gulls with their winding paths
tulip and May flowers in the garden.
My hands hold nothing
the night sky
clutching a few stars.
You were here once
and there is a dead space you left.
And I have said
nothing and known nothing
just as the tree says nothing
and knows nothing
but feels the wind
move about,
through leaves, branches.

Rain

Count rain on my fingers?
It is too fine,
like each column of pain—
the praying of pots
after washed,
put on the rack to dry.

The place where your death in February
connects with mine.

A swan
ruffling her feathers
after dunking

Her neck arched
orange bill shining.

Diana Gittins

Allotment

The thud of his fork in earth
the swish as she bends the branch
looking for what is hidden.

She reaches up and picks the hazels
as he lifts and lays potatoes
side by side in intervals of sun.

The apples she planted years ago
badly pruned, battle with bindweed
yet offer globes of ripened fruit.

She was alone then
hoping these might be
the ones that grew.

Mosquitoes, cabbage whites and pigeons
feast on skin
and hopeless broccoli

as the cardoon
spreading anarchically
festoons the sky with purple plumes.

Beethoven

He wears a dirty mac. His fingers
twitch and tap on his pensioner's pass
as stormy chords blow through the shelter
where he waits for the bus
that is so late
it drives him to write
a succession of string quartets
so ahead of their time a flotilla
of buses whizzes past unheard
heading straight for the depot
of another era.

Cathy Whittaker

Losing Her

I take her to the Art gallery by the river, it's a nightmare,
she will wander off and stare. You know that room with
the Rothko's, great big canvas's painted with bars of
thick colour look like trapdoors to me. She just sits on
a bench in the middle and watches them. Her body tense
with longing. Says she'd like to walk through the fiery red
rectangle into purple blue-grey, imagine she says, how
it would feel

falling,

it's time to go but she isn't listening, says that picture over
there the one with the orange over yellow, says she saw
the colours glow like the sun was crossing says she can see
angels in the gold hears them whispering. I say you'll be
talking to them next. It's time to go. All those huge spaces
holding smoke slowly burn crimson and black. Wake up,
snarl, but I can't see her. The yellow picture, the one she
said glowed,

 smiles,

Kill Me Pills
for Anne Sexton

you carried 'kill me pills' in your hand- bag
it must have reassured you when the night

dragged his teeth over your eyes

your slim ringed fingers must have lingered
on the warm brown glass

must have allowed you to sing out your poems
made each hour glow gold

as you were dragged into hospitals to doctors
who spread out your words like stepping stones

so you could find your numb way
back into the cage

allowed you home to watch trees
in your garden shiver

to grab the phone talk long distance

and still your father tapped his pipe
on the wall of your room

his musk- scented voice still trailed up the stairs

drifted into your bed as the cold-eyed night stared

it didn't matter that he was all shadow
he still stifled your screams

so you devised a new plan in that heat-heavy summer

locked yourself in the garage in your sleek- finned car
curled inside a mink coat of your mothers

sweating vodka-breath on the misting windows
you smoked yourself out

A Better Life
Cassandra Passarelli

'*Es mi hermana!*' she cries over and over, hands locked around her sister's throat.

To start with that's all Ula understands. Will nobody stop them? It's not her business. And yet...

The agency mothers gape: they're visiting San Antonio Aguas Calientes for an afternoon's shopping. None have known each other long, but removed from familiar surroundings they're more disposed to the solace of friendship. Shifting bureaucracy kept Mayans in place for centuries: these days it tyrannises everyone. Ula reckons she handles it better. Foreign cultures cannot be explained by common sense, she'd often advised her high-paying clients, you have to work with, not against, them.

But sense, common or otherwise, does not apply to Guatemala's adoption process. For six months Ula has been to and from the capital, trying not to breathe choking fumes or dwell on sprawling ugliness and millions of scuttling residents. She's been in and out of dusty government offices waiting for civil servants, seething with unspecified resentment, sign documents. Back and forth to immutable lawyers with stiff necks and piles of jaundiced folders, crammed with pages of dot-matrix text plastered with stamps. And always little Gorin in her front pack, bursting with bottles of formula, disposable diapers, scented wipes and toys. Yet no matter how hot or tearful Ula grew, Gorin maintained an equable tranquillity.

She was lucky, she reminded herself. Unlike many, she had decent Spanish. Her husband visited every couple of months or so. She was blessed with a mother, all the way from Sweden, to help. And the biggest break; Gorin was perfect. But, as they said at the agency, you got the child you deserved. With his pelt of jet hair and olive skin he was a charmer. As for his apathy, indigenous babies were inherently placid: whether nurture or nature was responsible, the agency mothers could only guess. Little Gorin was the finishing touch on a flawless life, centred on her career settling corporate ex-pats and a marvellous husband, heir to a publishing house; commitments which had kept her from having kids, but proved great reserves to draw on.

Her sole worry was Gorin's sublime indifference: Signild had noticed it. Typical of her mother to pick up on the significant detail, establishing her superiority at once. Ula didn't mention it to the agency mothers. She made a discreet appointment with an eye doctor in the City. He'd done the slit lamp test, the swinging flashlight exam and placed a headset on little Gorin. He mumbled something about poor pupil reactions: the lottery of adoption, malnutrition and Leber's Congenital Amaurosis. DNA tests were sent off and would be back within the week. In the interim, Signild's company irritated her. The only fallback was agency mothers, disorientated by the labyrinthine process.

'How quickly we women adapt,' she remarked to the post-feminist mothers, 'from being single to being in relationships, from having careers to being carers.' They smiled, unsure if she was complimenting or indicting them. Adaptation was, after all, the key both to survival and extinction.

She had accommodated: she was in good shape for a woman her age. But the caveat undermined the statement. She'd been passably pretty: blond hair, blue eyes, a good figure, the details hadn't mattered. A blousy ripeness that flamed and withered quickly. Now when she studied her reflection, all she saw was encroaching age: lumpiness where curves had been, cheeks marred by crows' feet. Like a page full of scrawls; an arbitrary lottery of doodles and crossings-out. It had been delightfully unpredictable at first, but contradictions set in. And all the while, Signild loomed large like some matriarchal archetype of a Norse myth, the spirit of venerable serenity. Preserved in a wintry spring, unwaveringly triumphant in her determination to grow old with dignity.

By her own account, Signild had given birth at forty-five, before the days of amniocentesis, labour barely interrupting lunch. She breast-fed till Ula could chew, yet had gone back to her job as a social worker in six weeks. Ula, perversely, hurtled towards middle age and was past childbearing at forty. Her body, once weightless and resilient, defied her: she understood it through its deficiencies. Unpredictable periods intensified, emotions atrophied into symptoms. Men's gaze rested on her less and fewer gentlemanly gestures were made now she hankered for them.

Then again, La Antigua wasn't such a bad place to hang out for half a year or more. Picturesque enough to fill a brochure several times over, surrounded by three volcanoes, ghostly earthquake ruins had lain in rubble undisturbed for two centuries. Neglect had preserved its colonial beauty better than Unesco might have. Restoration, with the affluent Ladino and visitor in mind, had smoothed rough edges. Too much polishing had burnished it to a fake lustre. Classy restaurants, hotels and discreet beauty salons glistened in its cobbled streets. Even by Minnesota's standards it was slick. If it was Guatemala you were after, rumour had it this wasn't the real thing. Ula was pretty sure she wasn't —but she didn't want her husband, arrived yesterday, to think adopting had dulled her sense of adventure.

But having Gorin had changed her. She hadn't suffered child birth, or the haze of suckling, but she was as tied to this child as much as the next mother. The occasional mood, serene Buddha though he was, demanded attention. His nappies and hunger, forethought. While she adjusted from executive to domestic, Alex was exploring the single life, second time around. No matter how mutual their considered decision was, she was in this leg alone. Of course he wanted to be there, but someone had to pay the agency's and lawyers' fees. She reminded herself this was a fleeting interlude. Soon she'd be back in Minneapolis's rat race, sending Gorin off to nursery, firing orders at the home help as she gulped down muesli.

So she'd invited the agency mothers to meet Alex, for a lunch and an outing. Signild was an angel—the perfect hostess. She made Kottbüllar and Janssöns Frestelse to go with the Akvavit. What she lacked as a mother, Signild made up for as a grandmother, baffling Ula. Alex had arrived in fine fettle. Separation had done him good; he was as attentive toward her as when they first met. As the guests came he introduced himself, managing to ask after a detail or two of their lives which proved he was listening on those long-distance calls.

There was Bessie, the stock broker, whose husband hadn't left Wall Street but sent a constant flow of exotic flowers and Swiss chocolates to keep her spirits up. And Estelle, the blond

New York liver specialist, adopting her second. The fat jolly Helena, a criminal lawyer, Lisbeth and Andrea. All top notch, professional women who'd got to a certain age and found it was too late. Clever women who'd accidentally or intentionally delayed. Some, noticing the frequency with which mothers are unhappy and grandmothers content, bypassed the prescribed biological window to the gateway to the golden years. Having spent fertile decades avoiding impregnation, latter ones were engaged with inducing it. Failing, they'd seized the chance to feel better about themselves by rescuing a child from an underdeveloped country.

But the defensive note that had crept into Ula's voice had not escaped Alex.

'It's incredible,' she told him on those late night calls, 'if you saw the conditions these kids are raised in, you'd die: in garbage dumps, in the street, in hovels with dirt floors and corrugated roofs. Running from one car to the next at traffic lights, selling Kleenex or phone cards. Mothers, unable to feed a first, have another and another. Fathers, drunks passed out cold in the street, start new families before the first has been weaned.'

Not so different from the ghettos in the city we call home, thought Alex, but he was new man enough not to contradict her.

'I want to come home,' she murmured. The locals made her feel queasy; fat women with gold teeth and plaits who never stopped smiling, men with sullen, closed faces. They only spoke to Ula to sell things. They were too many, here as at home: indistinct and dangerous.

'You always have to watch your wallet, hide your camera, not wear jewellery,' she told Alex. As she had been told. Six thousand murders last year: many victims of domestic violence. Not the sort a baby should be exposed to.

'Take Gorin's birth mother,' (that's what they call them at the agency) 'this unmarried girl, practically a child, pretended Eber,' (as Gorin was christened) 'was her sister's, to avoid church censure.' But, unable to feed him, she gave him up. The agency offered Ula the chance to meet Eber's aunt, but she'd decided against it.

She hadn't admitted, even to herself, the reason. Supposing the birth mother wanted Eber back when she saw Gorin.

Having never had one of her own (abortions didn't count) she could only guess at that umbilical bond Signild spoke of fondly. And never mind the birth mother's response, suppose Gorin betrayed some special affection toward her. It would break Ula's heart. For this reason, lawyers were paid, intermediaries' palms greased and endless papers signed and stamped. So that Ula, not the birth mother, was recognised as Gorin's one and only.

The luncheon went well. The women chatted and cradled dark-eyed babies. Toddlers gurgled and splashed in the fountain. The creepy Texan guy, whose wife was sick, brought his precocious foster-child and had inappropriate conversations with girls old enough to listen. They polished off two bottles of Akvavit, all of Signild's delicacies and bellowed out a traditional Swedish drinking ditty. Then they clambered into the hired minibus for San Antonio Aguas Calientes and bounced along a pot-holed road to the highway that curled up a mountain and down into a mess of grey breeze-block and rusty roofs. The driver pulled up to the artisans' market and slid back the doors.

The plaza was charming, with a stone fountain and bare whitewashed church filled with candles and flowers. The municipal building was decked with orange balloons and huge tarps printed with photos of the presidential candidate: a greying ex-general, fist raised. Men in orange t-shirts were inflating huge paper balloons with electric fans. They filled them with hot air till, billowing, they let them go. Kids watched as they drifted toward the mountains and lost colour. Without a backward glance, Alex strode into the square, undoing his camera case as he went.

The agency mothers unfolded their three-wheel prams or slung on their front packs and hesitated on the steps between the brilliant sunshine and the market gloom. Inside, weavers knelt on the floor, looms belted to their waists at one end and to pillars at the other. The agency mothers dispersed in twos and threes, filling the expanse with enthusiasm at wares covering every conceivable inch of wall, comparing prices. Ula felt unease ricochet around the room. She hung back, conscious of the contradiction of the babies' Mayan features with the agency mothers' Western ones.

'What a pretty girl you are. With curls too! How old?' she asked a child sitting on the steps, playing with a stuffed doll.

'Five,' a fine-featured mother, from the first stall, answered reluctantly.

'What's your name, *nena*?'

'Monica,' answered her mother, hovering between resentment and the instincts of a saleswoman.

'My boy's called Gorin.'

'Guatemalan?'

'Yes.'

'From where?'

'I don't know exactly... the orphanage – Hermano Pedro.'

A small group of weavers gathered around Ula, cooing and calling to Gorin in terse Cakchiquel. One, a particularly slight woman, bent down and kissed his forehead. Ula had heard of child-kidnappers lynched in Kiché and of children, conceived in desperation, with the sole intention of selling them. Of babies snatched from mother's arms as they waited for a bus or pickup. She gave a nervous smile and tried to push on, but the weavers surrounded her. The agency mothers were climbing stairs to the balcony in search of bargains, others were already outside, purchases tucked under their arms. Alex was in the square, taking photos. Flustered, she gripped Gorin tightly: he began to cry. She pulled free and sank down on the entrance steps, heart hammering. Signild appeared, smiling broadly with a garish bedspread destined to look out of place in the ashen tones of her Stockholm apartment.

Ula surveyed the square; the statue of a woman pouring water, communal *pila,* figus and tamarind trees. She'd lived here six months and understood little.

Monica's fine-boned mother walks briskly toward her, arm in arm with a young girl. The young girl is dressed in *traje,* skin patchy with malnutrition, dark circles beneath eyes that stare, unwavering, beyond the village into the mountains. Everything slows for Ula. They stop a few inches in front of her. Monica's mother guides the blind girl's hand to Gorin's face. She traces his profile with her fingers and runs them through his thick hair. Her expression of disbelief transforms into one of horror. Ula braces herself. The girl says nothing and pushes past her. Signild smoothes the bedspread on her lap:

'I knew you wouldn't like it, but I wanted a bit of Guatemala to remind me of my stay.'

Alex, who's sat down between them, is editing digital photos. He reassures Signild, half-heartedly, the bedspread will add warmth to her place.

The blind girl disappears behind them. The church bells ring out, timpani crashing and reverberating. As soon they die, a brass band starts a funeral march, drawing the straggling agency mothers onto the street to watch. Women sway single file on the left, men to the right, the silver and bronze coffin swinging on their shoulders.

All at once, from inside the market, comes a terrible commotion: shuffling, slapping and shrieking. Ula turns to see the blind girl dragging another by her hair. By the time they're in the street, the elder's plait is undone, her *huipil* loose: she whimpers, head tucked under like a roosting bird, doesn't retaliate. By now, everyone is watching.

'For goodness sake, somebody stop them!' cries Lisbeth.

'How awful!' screams Bessie.

But they all stand as still as the statue of the water carrier.

'*Mi hermana. Es mi hermana.*' My sister, my sister.

Ula hears the blind girl's anguish before she understands the words. Accusation or justification, she can't make out which: the girl is hysterical. She repeats herself, over and over. Ula puts it together.

'You said he was dead. You lied, how could you lie to me, *hermana*? You told me he was swept away by the river. I believed you... is that the way to treat your own sister? While I was grinding maize to bring in a few *quetzalitos*, you sold your own flesh and blood, like he was a basket of *tortillas*. That's where the money came from for the stove and the *lamina* roof. *Mi hermana!*'

'He was going blind... I knew. *Ala gran!* We couldn't keep another.'

Ula lets go of her front pack to seal her palms over her ears. A low moan drowns out the invective before she realises it came from her own mouth. Upset by his birth mother's screaming or Ula's wail Gorin, or is it Eber, begins to bawl again. The agency mothers are just getting to grips with what's happening when the driver grabs Ula's arm and bundles her into the minibus, shooing the others after.

The blind girl lifts her face at the slam of the sliding door. The driver starts the engine. As he shifts into first, she comes toward them, cheeks stained with tears and eyelids swollen. She scratches at the glass:

'*Mi hijo, mi hijo, mi hijo.*' My son, my son, my son.

The driver steps on the gas and accelerates out of the square.

Ula's breath mists the window. She's conscious of Alex at her side and her mother's hand, hovering on the headrest. She doesn't want to speak to them. She stares out at the village.

Stories are what you make of them. For the first time since she's arrived things make sense; she sees clearly. All is calm, defined. The cracks in the *adobe* walls over which fuchsia bougainvillea blossom spills. The gloss of lime tree leaves, branches heavy with fruit. Children, breathless with laughter, chase a chicken in a yard. An old man in Wellington boots, dwarfed by a bundle of cilantro tied to his back, descends a rocky path. Farmers in white shirts and straw hats, *machetes* dangling from their belts, cycle up the incline. Beyond, lie *milpas* that divide the absurdly steep, green mountains into neat handkerchiefs of land. The sky, too bright to look at, is hung with story-book clouds mingling with the smoke rising from the volcano.

Things Gorin will never see.

She looks down at him staring contentedly into space. At least in America no one will sell him, she tells herself. At least he'll learn to read Braille and go to a special school. At least he'll have a better life…

Bill Trüb

Lighthouse

Seems like yesterday we were stabbing little plastic boats with sticks of dynamite. I forget which one of us said, "You sunk my battleship," but I remember the game was over and you backed the Cadillac down the driveway. I watched from the bay window as you drove to the end of our street and turned into the wharf. You didn't check the rearview. I was eleven with the beard of a wise man.

None of that matters now—I'm spiralling up the 199 steps of Cape May lighthouse with a steel chain looped around my waist, an anchor hooked at the other end. It thrashes the helix of steps and shoots metallic chills up the lighthouse's spine...out the top of its head...across the Atlantic. I reach the top landing and blink the light frantically. Can't you see my flailing, silhouetted arms? You've forgotten something!

But you remain at sea. And the links are digging so deep into my hipbones, Dad, I think I may break in half.

Nové

He was born in a speeding taxi
during a blizzard so frigid
the snow angels flew south.

The cab whizzed beneath red stoplights,
sliding on asphalt slicked by black ice,
through a tunnel that unhinged its jaw.

Landmarks lashed past. A blur
of town hall, snippets of Main St., flashes
of the primary school and a porn shop.

His mother screamed like a Salem girl
on fire, her legs wishboned in the back seat,
chest heaving as she puffed, pushed, popped.

The boy's first blanket was a floor mat,
and he was nearly named after the cabbie,
Nikolay, who, disturbingly, smelt of vodka.

So the mother named her son November,
Nové for short. He grew up to be a doctor
or a race car driver or an angel. No one's sure.

He left home as a teen, believing he was
some broken boomerang flung into this wild
world on a whim, not meant to return.

And in some ways he was broken. He never knew
his father, his first dream was a nightmare,
he feared heights, depths, even the middle ground.

And now his mother does little but peer out
the peephole and windows, expecting one day to hear
a soft knock. Her door is always unlocked.

Bazaar

Duct-taped beneath a Romanesque archway, the devil-red banner boasted: *Our 3rd Annual Charity Bizarre! January 21st! Basement of St. Agnes' Church!*

The misspelling went unnoticed as parishioners, housewives and cutthroat senior citizens haggled over tricycles and garden gnomes, an ottoman, a broken Victrola—anything they didn't need and would never use. An overwhelmed woman bought two left-foot galoshes. A deaf boy hugged his brand-new, used flute. Newlyweds got a bargain on a king-sized mattress with queen-sized sheets.

I rummaged through a ghost-faced couple's collection of unusual boxes. All kinds—a mailbox shaped like a mallard, a hatbox from the Fifties, a jack-in-the-box to startle a child, an invisible box to trap a mime, a voice box to trap a scream. Next to me, a man in drag—may have been Father McClanahan—struck the deal of the day, an unbeatable 2-for-1 offer on a box spring to plant the pop of Agnes and a lunchbox to hide her cherry in.

Williamette

Inside our father's womb,
my brother broils
for four and a half months.
A half-boy, undercooked
but unbreakable.

Umbilical cord of barbed wire,
wrought iron wrists, *Made in America*
branded on his bottom.
A backbone of Pittsburgh steel,
pigskin, a lisp-proof tongue
and thunder in his hair.

Not one teardrop.

He grows into a quarterback
who grunts in huddles then launches
a Hail Mary just before a blind-spot tackle
plants his heart deep in Astroturf.

But me or Holden C.
will be open in the end zone
with crazy glue and deft hands
to complete the pass, win the Bowl
and harvest his heart,
that spit-shined, brazen-blue,
most masculine muscle.

Parklife
Kenneth Paul Stephen

Camille sipped her Volvic sport, licked her lips, then put the bottle down on the park bench and started to identify the first of the day.

He was tall with a beige, short-sleeved shirt. His dog sent pigeons into the air. He had a relationship walk so she turned to another- a male probably in his late twenties wobbling erratically on a bike. He was very much like Youssef from Marrakech, she thought. As he wheeled past, squeezing intermittently on his brakes, she imagined spreading thick dark paint on the palette. Such interest in that face. Yes, he would have been ideal. 'Excuse me. Did you run over a necklace back there, on the path? I think I might have broke it when...' The words didn't materialise and he cycled on.

'Oh, don't be too hard on yourself,' she thought. Had mother not worn that saying out, she might have heeded its meaning instead of just repeating words. Someone of her mother's generation couldn't imagine how to get on in this profession. Behind each tinted window of a newspaper office, a hidden bastard. They savaged her last exhibition. She borrowed money to make sure they all had champagne on preview night. She wore a low cut dress, talked to them about children she would never meet; smiled until she felt her cheek muscles spasm. Two days later, a boy laid out trays of bananas and grapes in white paper. It was barely seven. The stacks of newspapers sat in delivery plastic. He opened the string-wrap with a distended knife flick, tutting at her.

She opened the paper in the park, missing it. Then she saw it, tucked beside the small ads. 'Hyped artist misses cut.' She burst into tears, whacking a plastic bin. Trudging back, hiding her moistened eyes from the joggers, she wanted to go home, work in a shop, get fat and married prematurely. She resented her mother for entertaining her stupid dreams; hated and wanted her, like now.

Feeling her way over the grass, her legs felt weak. They were still her legs, supple, much admired in her aqua shorts. But she had less confidence in them. Fallen cones by the trees caused her ankles more discomfort than they should. Back home, she put Sigur Ros on her iPod and ran the bath.

Corran left six days ago, as he was meant to. This was the first time she had ventured out. Everything felt tender. Head, neck, even the discs in her back. None of which she had used much in the short time they were together. That was the funny thing.

For the last six days, she had left her curtains drawn. She knew it was light outside because she could see daylight, hinting through the thin fabric. Three brushes stood hardening in a glass, as dry as the skin on her scalp. His two portraits rested against the wall in the hall. The first- her interpretation of the person she had met in the park-was finished. Stubbled face, oddly feminine in cheekbone structure, with raven eyes peering below a black hooded top. That was the Corran she took in and cleaned up and learned the things he had done.

'No, not anything like that,' he said, flinching as she pressed the cold cloth against his cut eye. 'Territorial stuff.'

'And how do you get like this?' she asked, turning and folding the rag which was warming with his blood. 'I run,' he said. 'Mostly.'

He wasn't a good sitter. 'A boy from a restless house,' she thought. Intuition told her she should persevere, though; that it might be worth it. When she finished the first portrait, she felt relieved they had managed to get through it together. She ached a little. It had taken more out of her than the others.

'Hey sticky fingers,' she said, catching him picking at a blot of drying paint as she returned from the kitchen. He jumped at being caught unaware. She felt she should put him out of his misery, passing him an opened can of lager. She pretended to slap the back of his hand. They both laughed.

'It is good,' he said, tipping his head towards the finished portrait. He sipped his can. She lowered her foot, slowly, realising they were both leaning identically against the wall, opposite each other in her untidy hall.

'You are a good subject,' she said, taking his lager and swigging before giving it back. 'You can come back soon.'

She didn't shop, didn't like to, but she bought a new top. She considered wearing it for him coming but checked herself.

It was the first time she realised how easy it would be to abuse what she was doing. She pulled it back over her head, putting on a sweater which covered her arms, and concentrated on the light. She permitted herself a dab of perfume; pushed two bean-stained plates under the couch.

'I don't really know you. Tell me about yourself,' she said, after positioning him. She didn't look up, working an outline of his face in pencil.

'Does it matter to you?' he asked. He caught her off guard. She didn't want him to think her dishonest but she didn't want him to leave.

'I don't think I would be true to you if I didn't get to know you a bit,' she said. 'I want to capture the real you. When two strangers meet, something alters.'

He shook his head but stopped, politely, realising she had started to sketch again.

'You're mad, you know. You could get hurt doing this. I could have been anyone in that park.'

'That is true. I don't think you are, though. Just anyone, I mean.'

'Do you do girls?'

She gave a sarcastic smirk. 'I don't think the critics would see anything daring in that.'

'How many others? Men, I mean?'

'A few,' she said, lying.

He started at the beginning. 'They built the tenements facing south. At least they gave us some sunshine on the east coast of Scotland.'

She liked to listen to his voice. It had a rare timbre. He spoke of fears- so many fears. All those people in the park, different shapes- all of them full of fears. How vulnerable and she so strong, with that brush, capturing all that. Surely the critics would consider it bold.

'If I am ever in a bad place, I pretend to be someone else,' he said.

'I did it first when I moved school and got bullied. I remember, curled up, seeing boots flying. I was Muhammad Ali. It wasn't my pain, it was Ali's.'

She turned the water off with her foot and lay back in the foam. He would be walking around some street now, amongst architecture she didn't know, with his retro hold-all. People might look at him as if he was lost- and she could understand- but they wouldn't have it right. 'There you go again,' she thought to herself, 'pretending to know him.' He looked less lost with her, that was fact. That was what was meant to happen. The paintings were a record- a short meeting of unconnected people. Before and after. Corran's after-shot was incomplete. She was paying now for her procrastination.

'You need a new perspective,' he had said. She remembered the excitement in those eyes. 'Have you seen someone free-run?'

She didn't know the neighbourhood. He pointed to a cluster of three run-down business blocks. They went in a lift to the top. 'Where are we going?' she asked.

'Sshh,' he said.

He pulled her through a door by a recess at the top and they stepped out into the evening air.

'Wow.' She walked carefully to the wall and looked over. Then she stepped back, feeling dizzy.

'You ok,' he asked.

'Yea, fine. I think. What you doing?'

He was taking off his tracksuit top, stretching his arms and legs. He smiled at her. Then he turned and started to run towards the edge.

'Corran! Corran, look out.'

He got to the wall and she saw him jump. His body soared. His arms rose above his head. His legs arched upwards. For a moment, he was framed in mid-air, against the urban sky. Then gravity took him and pulled him down. 'Corran!' She darted to the side, bringing her hands to her face as if she couldn't look. She saw his body. He landed and rolled on the roof of the opposite block. The wind was blowing hair in her eyes. She swept it back, just in time to watch him stand up, cleanly, unbroken. He waved over. 'I'll come and get you,' he shouted.

Shivering on the wall, she still couldn't believe it. Her heart made her body shake like a frightened bird. 'I thought you were some sort of suicidal maniac. Don't do that again.'

'Sorry, it's what I do,' he laughed, knowing she would be scared. 'Here, you're cold.'

He offered his track suit top. She hated the cold. The top was at least four sizes too big. The smell was like the boy deodorants her brother used to wear. The familiarity made her feel safe. His hands moved slowly around her shoulder then came down to meet at her stomach. 'I'll zip it up for you,' he said. Inside she felt like she could gasp for air. She felt his warmth and might have rested her face on his arm, but she didn't know, and the moment passed. 'It's like rising out of yourself,' he said, looking over at the tower blocks. 'It's just you against the obstacle. Nothing else matters. Just you and that fraction of time.'

They sat quiet for a bit. If she knew it was right, she could have revived the moment by touching his arm. Part of her wanted to. Part of her feared losing her power.

'Come on,' she said, rising. 'I think I know what to do with you.'

'Take your top off,' she said, back at hers. She made him mimic the jump again in her living room. 'I'll get it this time,' she said, laughing.

The rug kept slipping. He fell twice, once knocking his head off the coffee table. She sketched the muscle, the stretched sinew. Tried to capture the concentration.

'Camille, I've had real fun,' he said.

It was the abruptness. The laughter making way for silence. She supposed the laughter might never stop.

'You're going?'

He looked down at a fallen coaster on the carpet.

'Yes.'

She scratched at the corner of the canvas, making marks.

Suddenly, it made sense. The roof. He was testing her. 'When are you going? I mean where?'

'Manchester,' he said. 'Tomorrow. I can coach there. I have a friend. It's money.'

She didn't know what to say or do with her body.

'Look, I can stay for a bit, if... It's just, I thought, well, this is about strangers meeting then, moving on, isn't it? he said.

She felt her voice breaking up. 'Yes.'

She looked up and saw that he was staring at her, as if waiting for her to tell him there was more.

'Look, what do you want me to say?' she shouted, throwing her pencils on the floor. She rushed to the bathroom and locked the door.

It felt surreal, like it never happened. She kept going to the window and looking out. She went back to the portrait. She would have to finish it now, while she could remember. Otherwise, it would all have been wasted. But she couldn't. She couldn't bear to touch it.

The park was cooler when she ventured out again the next day. She was conscious she had lost so much time. She had stayed in the bath until her album played through twice. She got lost in mindless television. Now she realised time was moving away from her. She examined her paintings in the cellar before she left. Another one, she reckoned, would do. She couldn't bear any more after Corran. 'Just get it done,' she thought. 'Just get the work away.'

He caught her by surprise as she sat down to assess the possibilities. 'You're here a lot aren't you?' she looked at him quizzically. 'Sorry. Do we know each other?'

'No, I'm Peter. You get to know faces. I am one of the rangers.'

She thought for a minute, thought of the ease of it. Then she explained.

'Look,' she said. 'I paint.' She was surprised, again, how little persuasion was required, just some chat, a flattering pair of shorts.

They agreed to meet at the ranger house when he finished at 5. She had always wanted to see inside that building. Walked past it often. An innocent enough mistake.

'I've seen you,' he said. He locked the door. It was just them. 'You go with men.' And the fracturing pain in her jaw felt like it split her open. She remembered the hardness of the floor. That was all, until she coughed awake into bitter cold. Her torn clothes felt wet. She pulled whatever she had, close. She couldn't see. The circulation in her numb, swollen hands and feet was cut off by rope. It was the darkness. The thought of rats; things crawling. She guessed she must have been below floorboards. She screamed as hard as she could but the pain in her jaw made her wince and shot pain through her back. She closed her eyes and cried. At least the darkness behind her eyelids was her own. She willed herself with all her strength to fall asleep. 'Mother, find me. Mother, I am here.' She shivered too much to sleep.

God knows how long she lay sobbing in that pit. She thought of touching her mother's face. She thought of home, of seeing light again. She thought of all the things she should have done. Stupid, stupid. 'Please make me warm, make me warm.' *Whenever I am in a bad place, I pretend to be someone else.* She could hear Corran. That beautiful voice. She thought of his hands, draping his track-suit top round her shoulders. Such a simple act. She remembered the smell. It made her warm, again. She rested her head against his arm, like she should have done. She liked that Camille better.

It was being that other Camille that kept her alive enough until, three days later, they heard her moans and uncovered the hatch.

'I need to go home, now.'

'It's OK,' they whispered, wrapping her in blankets. Something firm took the weight of her head. The ambulance lights hated her eyes. 'Hospital first, then home. Where's home? 'a lady asked.' Manchester. Please. Take me to Manchester.'

Contributors

Viccy Adams

Marion Ashton works part-time as an English Advisor for an international geological consultancy firm, shuttling between home in Lincolnshire, and Houston, Texas. Her poems have appeared in several magazines, including *Smiths Knoll, The North, Mslexia* and *Ambit*. She is currently working on an MA in Creative Writing with Royal Holloway.

Linda Benninghoff

Sharon Black is originally from Glasgow but now lives in the remote Cévennes Mountains of southern France. She runs a holiday retreat offering courses that include creative writing. She recently won the *Envoi* prize and has had several poems published. Sushi, dancing and the music of Dar Williams are among her passions.

Kate Brown studied film directing at the National Film and Television School. Her films 'Julie & Herman' and 'Absolutely Positive' have been shown on television and at film festivals, worldwide. She writes prose as relief from film development hell. Many moons ago, she used to live in an ambulance.

Rachel Crowther

Jane Draycott

Lizzie Fincham was born in Gower and is married with two daughters. She is short-listed for Poetry Business Competition 2005 judged by Simon Armitage, with two poems short-listed for Bridport 2009 judged by Jackie Kay, a poem highly commended by Carol Ann Duffy for Silver Wyvern 2009 and has won first prize in Barnet Open 2006 judged by Fleur Adcock. She is studying for am MA at Royal Holloway with Andrew Motion as her tutor.

Diana Gittins is an associate lecturer in creative writing for the Open University and has published a poetry pamphlet, Dance of the Sheet, and four works of nonfiction. Recently she has had poetry and prose published in Tears in the Fence, 14, Weyfarers and had two poems anthologized in the 2009 Cinnamon Poetry Pamphlet competition.

Gavin Goodwin is poet from Newport, South Wales. His poems have been published in *Agenda*, *FIRE* and *Wordriver*, as well as the Cinnamon Press anthology, *Black Waves in Cardiff Bay*.

Graham High is widely published in poetry magazines with four small chapbook collections to date. He has combined a vocation as a visual artist with a career as an Animatronic Model Designer in the Film Industry working on such films as *Aliens, Babe* and the *Harry Potter* series. www.grahamhigh.info

Will Kemp studied at Cambridge and UEA, then travelled throughout Asia and South America, before working as an environmental planning consultant in Holland, Canada and New Zealand. Since becoming runner-up in the Keats-Shelley Prize 2006, he has had over fifty poems published and shortlisted in various national journals and competitions. He has been shortlisted for the Cinnamon Poetry Award three times.

Frances-Anne King graduated in Creative Writing, from Bath Spa University, with First Class Honours. Her poetry has been published in various journals including *Acumen, Agenda, Envoi,* and *The Rialto*. She was a finalist in *The New Writers* 2008 Short Poetry Collection Competition and has just completed a first collection.

Phil Madden lives in Abergavenny but travels extensively across Europe as a consultant supporting people with disabilities. His Poster Poems were recently exhibited at a gallery in Brussels. He is working on a book of poems and wood engravings about birds with the award winning engraver, Paul Kershaw.

Marion McCready lives in Dunoon, a small town on the Firth of Clyde, with her husband and two young children. She has had poems published on-line and in print in places such as The Edinburgh Review, Poetry Scotland and the Glasgow Herald. Calder Wood Press will be bringing out a pamphlet of her poems in 2011.

Jane McLaughlin has published poems in numerous magazines and anthologies including Cinnamon Press anthology *In the Telling*. Her story 'Emergency Action' was published in the Cinnamon Press anthology *Storm at Galesburg*.

Tonya Mitchell is the recipient of the Best of Ohio Writer award in fiction. Her work has appeared in Scribe Valley Publishing's anthology *Welcome to Elsewhere* and her historical fiction in *The Copperfield Review*. She lives with her husband and three boys in Cincinnati, Ohio and is currently at work on a novel.

Sue Moules published two poetry collections last year: *In The Green Seascape* (Lapwing) and *Mirror Image* (Headland) with Norma E Jones. She is a founder member of Lampeter Writers' Workshop and chairman of Teifi Writers. Elin ap Hywel wrote of her work in Mirror Image, 'her work is delightfully aware of the numinous beyond the everyday.' She has been published in Poetry Wales, Planet, New Welsh Review, Roundyhouse and The Interpreter's House. And a previous Cinnamon anthology *The Ground Beneath her Feet*.

Padraig O'Morain's poetry has been published in magazines which include Ambit, The Rialto, The North, Magma, Poetry Ireland Review and Cyphers. His pamphlet *You've been great* was a winner of the Poetry Business Award in 2007. His published poetry can be read at www.padraigomorain.blogspot.com He lives in Dublin with his wife and two daughters.

Cassandra Passarelli lives in a rainforest village in Guatemala where she runs a children's library. Born in London, she ran a bakery for ten years, managed a charity, sub-edited and wrote theatre reviews. She's travelled in the Middle East, West and East Africa, Latin America and Sri Lanka and studied literature, journalism and creative writing. She won the jam session at the Traverse Theatre's Debut Authors Competition and was shortlisted for RRofihe Trophy, Happenstance, Wells Festival Story Prize, Cadenza, SFWPLA and Aesthetica Creative Works competition. She has been widely published and her novella *Greybill* is published by Skrev.

Marina Sanchez is a published poet and translator. Of Native American/Spanish origins, she was brought up in Europe. She likes dancing, water, mangoes and standing on her head. She abhors liars, bores and winter. One day she would like to grow orchids.

Amy Shuckburgh's stories have been short-listed for the Bridport Prize, the Bristol Prize and the Fish Short Story Prize. Amy is both a writer and a portrait painter. She lives in London with her husband and daughter.

Eabhan Ní Shuileabháin, daughter of an Irish-American father and an Irish mother, grew up in Dublin, Ireland, but now lives in Gwynedd, Wales, with her husband and son. Her poetry has appeared in numerous journals throughout Europe and America.

Kenneth Paul Stephen is an emerging voice in Scottish fiction. He grew up in a village called Padanaram, which had no shop. One day, a mobile library van drove through and he discovered the wonders of fiction. In May, he won the David Toulmin short story prize.

Lynne Taylor has written four novels, unpublished, and a couple of hundred poems, some of which have been published in anthologies and literary magazines. Her fundamental fascination is what makes people tick and how they affect one another. Writing, for her, is a kind of therapy. It's like acting on paper. She lives the character. And therefore explores herself.

Aisling Tempany was born in Ireland in 1985. She grew up in Lancashire and was home-educated until she was 16. Since 2003, she has lived in Wales. Having graduated from Cardiff University in 2009, Aisling will be studying for an MA in Wales on Welsh and Irish writing.

Bridget Thomasin has lived in the same valley on Dartmoor for 29 years and her poetry and painting celebrate this unique place and the surrounding moorland.

Bill Trüb is a writer from coastal New Jersey. His poetry has been anthologized in *Your Messages* (2008) and *The Review of Contemporary Poetry* (2005), both published by bluechrome. Bill holds a Master's degree with distinction in creative writing from Cardiff University, and has performed his work in the UK and the US. He was poet-in-residence on a popular university radio show in Wales. Currently, he is the senior editor for a business magazine located near New York City. He is 26 years old.

David Underdown was born in England but has spent much of his life in the West of Scotland. For the last ten years his home has been the Isle of Arran in the outer Clyde where he lives with his wife, grows vegetables and tries to catch up on his reading. A number of his poems have appeared recently in anthologies and journals. Some can be read at www.davidunderdown.com. His first full collection, Time Lines, will be published by Cinnamon in 2011.

Sue Vickerman had two poetry collections published (Arrowhead Press, Biscuit Publishing) while living in a Scottish lighthouse. Some of her stories have been anthologized (Virago, Diva Books, etc) and her novel *Special Needs* will be published by Cinnamon in 2011. Home is wherever she lays her hat—currently a room in a watermill in the Yorkshire Dales.

Lyn White's work has been published in a variety of journals and anthologies. She is a member 'the common room poets' who workshop at the University of Kent at Canterbury. Their first anthology, *Circled Like a Target*, appeared in 2004, their second, Mirror Writing in 2009.

Cathy Whittaker has had her poems published in many magazines and anthologies. She was the Warwick Poet Laureate for 2008/9. She works as a Creative Writing tutor, and co-founded openmindwriting.com which offers workshops and courses for writers. She is currently working on a sequence of poems about the Lake District.

Martin Willitts Jr poems will appear in *Storm at Galesburg and other stories* (international anthology). His tenth chapbook is *The Garden of French Horns* (Pudding House Publications, 2008) and his second full length book of poetry is *The Hummingbird* (March Street Press, 2009. He is co-editor of www.hotmetalpress.nert